BECAUSE *I Said* FOREVER

EMBRACING HOPE IN A NOT-
SO-PERFECT MARRIAGE

DEB KALMBACH

and

HEATHER KOPP

MULTNOMAH
BOOKS

BECAUSE I SAID FOREVER
published by Multnomah Books

© 2001 by Debbie Kalmbach and Heather Kopp
International Standard Book Number: 978-1-59052-777-1

Cover design by The Office of Bill Chiaravalle
Cover image by Photonica
Interior images by Visual Language Library
Scripture quotations are from:

The Holy Bible, New International Version
© 1973, 1984 by International Bible Society,
used by permission of Zondervan Publishing House.

The Holy Bible, King James Version (KJV)

The Living Bible (TLB) © 1971.
Used by permission of Tyndale House Publishers, Inc.
All rights reserved.

Published in the United States by WaterBrook Multnomah, an imprint of the
Crown Publishing Group, a division of Random House Inc., New York.

For information:
MULTNOMAH BOOKS • 12265 Oracle Boulevard, Suite 200
Colorado Springs, CO 80921

Library of Congress Cataloging-in-Publication Data:
Kalmbach, Deb.
  Because I said forever / Deb Kalmbach & Heather Harpham Kopp.
    p. cm.
  ISBN 978-1-59052-777-1
  1. Marriage—Religious aspects—Christianity. 2. Wives—Religious life.
3. Wives—Conduct of life. I. Kopp, Heather Harpham, 1964- II. Title.
BV835.K356 2001
248.8'435—dc21
                    2001003166

146673257

For Randy—

husband, friend, God's miracle

Contents

Acknowledgments 7

Introduction: A Different Kind of Marriage Book 9

1. Why Are You Staying? 13

2. Denial Is a Two-Way Street 19

3. Can This Marriage Be Saved? 24

   Voices: Kim's Story 30

4. "About My Husband, Lord..." 33

5. What Was God Thinking? 38

6. When Your Bootstraps Break .43

7. What About Our Children? 47

8. The Mercy Blanket 53

9. Martyrs Anonymous 57

   Voices: Anne's Story 62

10. Bitter or Beautiful? 64

11. "My Name Is Pain" 70

12. Am I Devoted or a Doormat? 74

13. Drawing Lines with Love 79

14. Contentment—It Can Be Habit Forming 85

    Voices: Corrie's Story 89

15. Marriage Is Blind 91

16. When the Grass Looks Greener 96

17. I Surrender All 103

18. I Married a Fool 108

    Voices: Jackie's Story 115

19. Marriage as Ministry 118

Contents

20. "She Did It...Why Can't I?" 123

21. Who...Me? 129

22. Rethinking the *S* Word 132

23. Emotional Ping-Pong 137

24. Sleeping with the Enemy 142

25. Sex Matters 148

Voices: Kendra's Story 155

26. Too Busy to Believe 158

27. The Most Crushing Blow 162

28. Impossible Forgiveness 168

29. Angels 173

30. "I'm So Lonely!" 176

31. Getting a Life 180

Voices: Darlene's Story 184

32. Emotional Baggage 187

33. Choosing Obedience 192

34. "I Was Wrong" 196

35. Should We Separate? 200

36. Friendly Support 205

37. Smart Ways to Sway Him 209

Voices: Twyla's Story 215

38. One Day at a Time 218

39. Promise Centered 222

40. When It Hurts to Hope 226

41. Amazing Grace 230

Appendix: Hard Questions .... .235

1. What should I do if my husband hurts me physically?

2. What should I do if my husband is addicted to alcohol or drugs, and he won't get help?

3. At what point do my husband's verbal barbs become emotional abuse?

4. What if my husband refuses to be responsible to work and support our family?

5. How can I know if my husband is molesting my kids, and if he is, what should I do about it?

6. What if my husband suffers from a mental illness or chemical imbalance but won't seek treatment or stay on his medication?

Acknowledgments

I have struggled to know how to put into a few words the huge amount of gratitude I have for everyone who helped this book come to life. It was a true community effort!

Without the encouragement of my coauthor, Heather Kopp, my book proposal probably would have sat in a slush pile on some editor's desk with my rejection file growing. Thank you, Heather, for your heart for this project, and for your countless e-mails, phone calls, votes of confidence, and long hours of writing and editing. You have been a tireless advocate, a tremendous coach, a treasured friend. I am grateful beyond words.

Working with Multnomah Publishers has truly been a privilege. David Kopp—senior editor, friend, and encourager of writers—has cheered me on through the years. Thank you for believing in possibilities and encouraging Heather and me behind the scenes.

My editor, Liz Heaney, was a tremendous and indispensable help during the revision process. Thank you for helping us deliver the very best book we could.

A big thank-you to Marlee Alex, who contributed greatly to the appendix questions.

To Elaine Colvin and Colleen Reece, mentors and friends, thank you for all you have taught me about writing and life.

Thank you to my forever friends. You have been so much a part of this story. You have sat with me in support groups, comforted me, prayed with me, and given me hope. Your voices resonate through the pages of this book and in my heart always. A sincere thank-you to Mary, Twyla, Connie, Judy, and Coni for boldly telling their stories. You are loved and appreciated.

To my faithful brothers and sisters in Christ at Wabash Church in Auburn, Washington, and at Friendship Church in Winthrop, Washington, for never giving up, for always believing, persevering, and praying. Thank you for being there for Randy and me.

To the Kalmbach and Fisher clans, our parents, brothers, and sisters, who always stood by us and loved us, for better, for worse. You have blessed our lives.

To Chris and Jeremy, our precious sons. Thank you for loving your parents in spite of their imperfections. You have brought inexpressible joy to our marriage and family.

My deepest thanks to my husband, Randy. Your support and encouragement to write our story is yet another gift from the Lord, evidence that He does work all things out for good.... Your courage is an inspiration to me. I love you forever!

Introduction:
A Different Kind of
Marriage Book

I remember the day as if it were yesterday—a hot, humid, late-July afternoon. The fragrant rain-scent from a thunder-shower lingered, but nothing could spoil our near-perfect day, not even rain.

Randy and I stood at the altar; three hundred well-wishers filled the church. Sixteen bridesmaids and ushers surrounded us, and my two youngest brothers held hands timidly, guarding our rings on pink dotted-swiss pillows.

Randy and I were only nineteen. (When our own sons turned nineteen, I shuddered as I realized how young and immature their father and I had been at that same age.) But we promised to love, honor, and cherish each other in sickness and in health, for better or for worse.

Little did either of us realize that "worse" would mean searing emotional pain, deep conflicts, and an endless series of crushing disappointments.

Shortly after Randy and I were married, he began to drink heavily. At first I rationalized his behavior—he drank because of pressure from coworkers, stress from his job, our two fussing toddlers, my inadequacies. Whatever the reason, I prayed I'd find a way to make him stop drinking.

Instead, his drinking escalated into full-blown alcoholism. Soon my every thought was focused on Randy and how I could "fix" him. But in spite of all my efforts and my love, he still drank. I saw him slowly slipping away from me, from our marriage, from life…

Whatever the circumstances of your marriage today, you probably began with stars in your eyes, like Randy and me. You had a wedding. You made promises to love, cherish, and honor. But then something went awry or maybe even drastically wrong. Maybe you have come up against what seems to be an impossible situation in your marriage. It might be alcoholism, illness, drug addiction, or a husband who works way too many hours at the office. Perhaps your husband vents his anger and frustration at you or your children unmercifully. He might retreat into his own world of thoughts, and you don't have any real emotional intimacy. Maybe he has been unfaithful to you multiple times.

In any case, your marriage today is not so perfect or far from perfect. The vows you exchanged during your ceremony seem unrealistic, even downright silly, in light of current reality. "For better or worse" sounds like an impossible cliché, and "forever" feels more like a life sentence than something to look forward to.

Maybe by now you feel jaded. You read a lot of Christian marriage books but couldn't identify with the couples discussed. The problems presented seemed trivial, the solutions simplistic and unrealistic. Even more disappointing, the authors seem to assume that both you and your husband share an equal passion for Christ and for making a great marriage. None of these books talked about what to do when your husband bellows unreasonable orders, thinks romance is for the birds, or is addicted to cocaine.

This book is different. Whether you are slightly dissatisfied with your marriage or near the end of a dead-end road, I pray it gives you reason to hope and ideas to transform your relationship with your husband. In these pages you will meet women like you, women who are committed to their marriages. Women who take seriously the vows they made before God. And like you they are looking, some desperately, for compassion and strength in the face of what feels like an impossible marriage.

Although the church discourages divorces, a recent study by George Barna indicates that Christian marriages don't fail as often as secular marriages—they fail more![1] I believe one reason is that too often the Christian wife who finds herself in a hard marriage imagines she has only two courses: gutting it out miserably but putting on a happy face or leaving the marriage feeling guilty and condemned.

This book says there's another way. The reflections you read here will affirm your decision to stay in your marriage. But they will also offer you encouragement and help for moving beyond simply enduring a bad marriage. You'll discover that it is possible to be personally fulfilled even if your marriage is not fulfilling. It is possible to discover joy, to find the support you need, to thrive in your spiritual life and Christian walk, and to turn your challenges into opportunities for personal and spiritual growth.

Some chapters offer practical insight on common problems, such as: How do I honor a husband who acts like a jerk? How do I know when to establish boundaries? Do I have to be a doormat? How can I improve our love life? Others will discuss what Scripture has to say about what it means to submit, the importance of forgiveness, and how to influence your husband to become a Christian. And still others focus on helping you to salvage your own inner joy, practice persevering love, and grow your faith in God even while you are in a marriage that may not ever become the one you dreamed of having.

I have been trying to write this book in some form or another for about ten years. It just wasn't God's timing. I had more to learn (and still do!), but the Lord opened doors I couldn't have imagined.

An old writing friend, Heather Kopp, read my proposal and contacted me, offering to coauthor the book. I was delighted. Her passion for encouraging and helping other women in difficult marriages equaled mine (Heather's first marriage ended in divorce). Someone once said, "You teach more with your scars than with your victories." That's what we bring to this book: scars from extremely painful, not-so-perfect marriages.

Although Heather wrote parts of this manuscript, for ease of reading she decided to be "invisible." So whenever you see the word *I*, it refers to me (Deb). On that note, I am grateful for my husband's encouragement and willingness to let me write freely about our story and our many mistakes. It's a story full of heartache, but also one that tells of God's ability to redeem even the most hopeless situations and marriages.

Because you said *forever* and meant it, though I have never met you, we are sisters. You aren't alone. And I'd love to hear how this book encouraged you or someone you know. Feel free to write to the address in the back of the book.

In the meantime, "Let us not become weary in doing good, for at the proper time we will reap a harvest if we do not give up" (Galatians 6:9).

Deb Kalmbach

one

Why Are You Staying?

*Because of the Lord's great love, neither my husband
nor I are condemned for our mistakes and failures.
In fact, God's love and compassion for us and our
marriage will never fail or become worn out. Every
morning His mercies for us are brand new. And
remembering this truth gives me great hope.*

A PARAPHRASE OF LAMENTATIONS 3:22–23

You've chosen to stay. Your family and friends think you're crazy, and you sometimes think, *Maybe they're right.* You're swimming against the current of popular opinion when you choose to stay in a not-so-perfect marriage. Society supports, even encourages, unhappy wives to bail. The rhetoric bombards us: "Why are you staying?" "You deserve to be happy." "You're getting short-changed." "No one expects you to stay—you made a mistake; now just move on with your life."

It's easy to fall into self-pity and to agree with the assessment that we deserve better. And in a real sense, we do deserve better than being in a marriage where we're taken for granted, belittled, or ignored.

But God's ways include a different set of standards than society's. We see this all through Jesus' teachings. He says we must lose our lives to find them, become poor in order to be rich, love our

> The world says quit—but ask God for staying power. For determination, patience, 'gutsy' courage to survive and survive well.
>
> ANNE ORTLUND

enemies—especially when we don't feel like it.

Mother Teresa once said, "It would be enough for us to remember that it is Jesus who gives us, through such a person or circumstances, the opportunity to do something beautiful for Him."[1] She referred to difficult people, even husbands, as being God's "distressing disguise." By choosing to stay in a difficult marriage, we have the opportunity to love our husbands as we love Jesus, to be the living expression of God's kindness.

You are inviting God to work in you and in your marriage if you have chosen to stay for any of the following reasons:

- Because you believe that God can and will help you to improve your marriage, even if your husband doesn't change.
- Because you believe that your marriage is a tool God will use to help you grow, mature, and become like His Son.
- Because you believe that God created marriage to last forever and you know that divorce breaks His heart.
- Because you believe that God will give you all the grace and strength you need in order to handle the challenges of a difficult marriage.
- Because you choose to love your husband in spite of his failings and faults.
- Because your hope for happiness and joy in life doesn't depend only on your husband or your marriage.

And while these reasons may sound noble and appealing, you know that in everyday life this kind of love translates into hard work. It means sacrificing certain rights, needs, and even some of your fondest dreams. It requires patience, perseverance, and a commitment bold enough to face down one bad day after another. Ultimately, it requires maturity.

Sadly, many wives who stay in not-so-perfect marriages do so for reasons that are less noble or spiritually demanding. They feel resigned to the status quo and don't seek something more, either for themselves or their marriages.

If that's you, you've decided to endure rather then enjoy your marriage. And you are missing out on what God could do—in you, if not your husband—if you really gave Him a chance.

If you've chosen to stay, it may be because...

You see no alternative; you feel trapped. It's easy to stay because you're too afraid to leave. How will you take care of your family financially, deal with loneliness, and overcome your guilt about going against God's command not to divorce unless your husband has been unfaithful?

These concerns are legitimate. But the problem with staying in your marriage because you feel trapped is that you can't begin to work constructively on your relationship. Your strongest impulse will be to get free, to escape. This puts you in danger of making destructive choices, having an affair, or driving your husband further and further away because you are seething with resentment about being in this prison.

If your marriage feels like a cage, the most important step is to realize that you are not trapped. God is not your jailer. He has given you a free will. He wants you to stay in your marriage because you choose to, not because you're convinced there's no way out. When we grab hold of this truth, it makes all the difference in our perspective.

Just ask Mary. The wife of a busy realtor in her small town, Mary says, "My husband Henry wouldn't go to counseling; he wouldn't talk; all he did was hang out with his buddies. What with a baby and no job or training, I felt trapped in our marriage. A friend stepped in and began to help me see how I could support myself, how I could make it work. She convinced me that if I really wanted to leave, I could. It was a revelation.

"But I didn't leave. Instead, for the first time I decided to stay not as a victim, not as a caged wife, but as a woman free to leave who instead has chosen to stay. It made all the difference in my outlook and in how I treated Henry."

For the children's sake. There's no denying that they should be part of a decision to stay (recent studies show that children fare better with parents whose marriage remains troubled but intact than they do in divorce situations).[2] Yet this should not be your driving reason to stay.

Why? Because if you remain married solely for the kids' sake, you are likely to invest more of your emotional energies and time in them than in your marriage. After all, you're just trying to keep the marriage intact until they're grown or can handle the trauma. But your kids will pick up on this and feel a certain amount of nameless guilt, sensing they are part of what's keeping you trapped. And you'll be less motivated to work on improving your marriage or putting your husband first—things that could truly help your relationship rebound.

You are comfortable being the victim, the martyr. Playing the role of a martyr has become part of your identity. It makes you feel good, even noble, to stay in a bad marriage. You enjoy the praise of others who look on and think, "What a woman!"

But just because something is comfortable or easy, it doesn't necessarily mean it's wise or good. This posture will likely lead to increased problems in your marriage as your husband gets used to this pattern and loses respect for you. Beware: If this is your reason for staying, you are at risk for someday waking up and feeling very, very angry.

To prove you are a good, strong Christian. God has more for us than to just gut it out in our marriages. He wants us to desire to please Him, to live lives worthy of His calling, to experience peace, contentment, even joy.

When a wife's goal is to prove that her faith is strong and that her commitment to obey God is remarkable, something else is probably going on too. She will have a hard time not slipping into the subtle noose of self-righteousness, which will only choke her love and drive her husband further away. When her stamina finally wears thin, she'll discover that she's been motivated by guilt and fear, rather than by sincerity and love of God and her husband.

Everyone else thinks you should stay. If you are staying because the majority of friends and relatives polled think you should, what will you do if the winds of opinion shift? It's not wrong to get input and advice from people we love and respect. But ultimately, a wife should base her decisions about her marriage on God's Word, His Spirit speaking to her, and the counsel of spiritual mentors or marriage and family professionals.

If you realize that you've been staying in your marriage for all the wrong reasons, ask God to help you see a bigger picture. Ask Him to free you—not from your marriage, but from your fears, from your sense of isolation and your perceived lack of options.

And prayerfully consider this thought. Zig Ziglar writes:

I have no way of knowing whether or not you married the wrong person, but I do know that many people have a lot of wrong ideas about marriage and what it takes to make that marriage happy and successful. I'll be the first to admit that it's possible that you did marry the wrong person. However, if you treat the wrong person like the right person, you could well end up having married the right person after all. On the other hand, if you marry the right person, and treat that person wrong, you certainly will have ended up marrying the wrong person. I also know that it is far more important to be the right kind of person than it is to marry the right person. In short, whether you married the right or wrong person is primarily up to you.[3]

And let me suggest that you go one step further. Say to yourself (and your husband) this week, "I'm staying in this marriage because I choose to. I am not here because I can't leave. I'm not here because of what others think. I'm not here to prove something noble about myself. I'm here because I believe this is the best place for me to be, that God has called me to be in this marriage and to do my best to love and respect you—no matter how challenging that is. I told you when we married that I'd stay with you forever. And that's a promise I plan to keep."

> *Dear God,*
> *I'm staying, but I want to do it for the right reasons. I need your help to sort through my motivations, so I avoid the pitfalls of being a martyr, coward, super-Christian, or use my children as an excuse. I need courage to love my husband in the way that I want to be loved and to stand firm in my convictions within a world that condones quick fixes and easy answers, even in marriage. Let me consider this possibility: I just might have married the right person after all! Amen.*

Two

Denial Is a
Two-Way Street

*Why do you notice every little sin in your husband's
life and pay no attention to the very substantial sins
in your own life? How can you say to your husband,
"Let me help you out with that problem you've got
there," when all the time there are even greater issues
and sins in your own life?*

A PARAPHRASE OF MATTHEW 7:3–4

Randy wasn't always a drinker. I met him at a sledding party in high school. We were just sixteen. We flew down the hill on a Flexible Flyer and landed in a snowbank, laughing and throwing snow at each other. His warm brown eyes and shy grin reflected his easygoing personality. It didn't take long for our relationship to grow, and we enjoyed all the hallmarks of being high school sweethearts: football games, proms, going to movies, falling in love.

But one weekend after graduation, Randy went camping with some of the guys and got drunk for the first time. "You should've seen me, Deb," he laughed. "I almost finished off a fifth of whiskey." I scolded him, and he vowed it wouldn't happen again. I loved him. I wanted to believe him. We got married the following summer.

Randy's drinking continued in college. Everyone went to fraternity parties where ample supplies of alcohol waited. After college graduation, when Randy joined the military, drinking became like a medal of manhood. I considered it harmless and didn't worry until I saw him changing. He began to spend more and more time at bars. He was always remorseful afterward. "I love you, Deb. I'm going to quit," he'd promise.

I clung to each word and searched for hope. Randy was usually gentle, sensitive, and a good provider.

But the drinking continued, and finally, after ten years of marriage, I could no longer deny that he had a drinking problem. The word *alcoholism* played in my thoughts, but I shrugged it off. Alcoholics were down-and-outers who sipped liquor from bottles disguised by crumpled paper bags, or so I thought. They slept under bridges and shuffled through town, dirty, smelly, unshaven, gaunt. Randy was anything but that. He was young, healthy, and held down his job responsibly. If I could somehow hang on to the illusion that everything was okay, then I could deny that he—we—had a problem. I didn't want to say the words, "Randy is an alcoholic. Our marriage is a mess. I am miserable."

It's hard to believe we can be so deeply entrenched in denial. Yet denial has been described as a shock absorber for our souls, a warm blanket we wrap ourselves in until we are ready to face reality and its subsequent pain. When we let go of our protective mechanism, then we are faced with the difficult dilemma—how do I handle these problems? What now? We will only take off the protective blanket when we're ready to tell ourselves the truth.

Pain finally pushed me beyond denial. The consequences of Randy's drinking were so blatant and disruptive that I could no longer pretend. He was in danger of losing his job, career—everything. My husband was an alcoholic.

Once I admitted that I had been in denial about Randy's alcoholism, I began to see that I'd also been in denial about areas I needed to change in myself. Though I didn't cause Randy's drinking and had painfully learned that I couldn't control or fix him, I was surprised to discover how much I had contributed to our problems. My biggest area of denial was believing that I played only a minor role in our problems.

It's not that I thought I was the perfect wife. Randy's offenses were just more obvious than my more subtle heart issues. I convinced myself that if he would change, if he would stop drinking, then our marriage had a chance. What I couldn't see was how I tried to manipulate and control him.

I made demands of him and had unrealistic expectations. I had expected him to be more open to becoming a Christian and to be more sensitive and romantic. I had expected him to act like my knight in shining armor. And I told him so. Often. I couldn't appreciate his good qualities because I had become so focused on the negatives. My self-righteous, superior attitude only made Randy feel worse. Many times I felt more like his mother than his wife, his partner, his best friend. I rarely told him in a loving way how I felt about his drinking and his withdrawal from our marriage and family.

Admitting that I had an equal stake in what our marriage had become was my first step in changing how I related to Randy.

It's easy for us to see another person's denial, but what about our own? Be careful that you aren't so focused on your husband's issues and his denial that you stop seeing yourself. It is hard to admit we have a habit or personality flaw we can't seem to kick or fix. It's even harder when we think our husband has a much more obvious one!

May I ask you some questions?

- How willing are you to face the truth about your marriage—and your part in it?
- Are you willing to ask your husband for input? Are you willing to ask him how he thinks you see him?
- How do you feel about your marriage today? Can you give an honest answer?

A friend of mine named Wendy spent many years denying that she had a jealousy and rage problem. Her marriage had been rocky almost from the start because she was preoccupied with her husband Steve's failure to find and keep a good-paying job. She blamed Steve's lack of ambition and lazy attitude for their unhappiness.

Wendy was so certain of Steve's culpability that she couldn't see that she also had contributed to their problems. Because her first husband had been unfaithful, she had always felt certain Steve would betray her too. She flew into a rage if she thought he was looking at another woman or if he even glanced at the provocative *Cosmopolitan* cover in the grocery store. Once Steve's chiropractor prescribed a massage, and the masseuse was female. When Wendy found out, she was so outraged and hurt, so sure that Steve had somehow derived sexual pleasure by having another woman touch him, that she slept in their guest room for two nights.

It wasn't until Wendy's marriage was in shambles and Steve had an affair that she finally accepted her part in the disintegration of the relationship. It wasn't her fault that Steve strayed, but her constant distrust of him had deeply undermined his own confidence in his ability to be faithful. It's been a long process of healing and forgiveness for Wendy and Steve. Wendy's willingness to own her part in their marital problems has opened doors in their relationship that she never could have imagined.

In a not-so-perfect marriage, rule number one is easy to miss: Don't deny your own contribution to your marital unhappiness.

Author Susan Page puts it this way:

> Are you ready to let go of the booby prize of being right
> and to dig for the gold of seeing your own role in your rela-
> tionship problems?…The reason your own role is gold is
> that you can do something about it. Though you have no
> control over your partner's opinions and behaviors, you
> have unlimited control over your own! Instead of saying to
> your spouse, "You change so we can be happy," you are
> now able to say, "I'm going to change so we can be happy."
> Do you feel the power in the second statement?[1]

The second you own your own part in your marriage problems, you'll have more hope that things can change because
although you can't change your husband, you can change yourself!
And what's more, as soon as you ask God to help you see what you
want to deny, He will come rushing to your aid to help you change.
"The very day I call for help, the tide of battle turns," wrote the
psalmist (Psalm 56:9, TLB). Let today be that day for you.

> *Dear God,*
> *Sometimes I feel so overwhelmed by our problems.*
> *Our marriage seems hopeless. Don't let me miss the*
> *potential for change in myself. Lord, where have I been*
> *wrong? Please give me courage to see the truth, to face*
> *my denial, to be willing to act differently. I know real*
> *change is only possible when I submit myself to You.*
> *Help me, Lord. I can't do this in my own strength.*
> *When I read Your Word, I realize the depth of Your*
> *love for me—and my husband. No problem is too big*
> *for You. No one is ever beyond Your reach. Amen.*

three

Can This Marriage Be Saved?

*Restore us, O God Almighty; make Your face shine
upon us, that we and our marriage may be saved.*

A PARAPHRASE OF PSALM 80:7

an This Marriage Be Saved?" is a regular feature in a popular women's magazine. Maybe you've seen it. First a therapist
fills us in on the husband's perspective on his ailing marriage. Then
we get the scoop from the wife. Often there's a glaring chasm
between the two views. The article concludes with recommendations and a prognosis. Sometimes the marriage simply can't be
saved and the couple parts.

Is there such a thing as a marriage that can't be saved, one that
is too far gone?

Molly thinks so. "My marriage is already dead," she states.
"There are no feelings of affection, much less romance. It's like we're
already divorced; we just haven't signed the papers or moved out
yet. It feels like I'm hauling around a dead body in the trunk of my
car, and I need to just admit it's there and dump it."

Sometimes a marriage like the one Molly is describing is in
deeper trouble than a marriage where two people are constantly

fighting. Where there is fighting, there is passion, emotion, and at least some connection between the couple. But where there is only a sense of deadness and neither spouse even cares anymore...how can you resurrect such a relationship? Is it even possible?

It might take a miracle, but that's what God is in the business of doing.

Experts tell us that a marriage can be brought back from the brink if at least one partner is willing to try, willing to invest energy and effort. Feelings can be reborn and affection restored.

If you identify with Molly but truly want to save your marriage, you need to make some conscious and dramatic changes—beginning with the decision to change almost everything about the way you relate to your husband. Decide that with God's miraculous power and help, you are going to do everything you can to resurrect this marriage. Tell your husband: "I want to save this marriage. I really want to try. I know that we both feel it's dead, a goner. But I also know that God can do miracles."

Ask your husband if he's willing to help. If not, don't let his disinterest dissuade you. Simply proceed on your own to make as many of these changes as possible:

Be willing to reengage emotionally. As unresolved conflicts and feelings pile up over the course of years in a marriage, partners gradually begin to harden their hearts. Maybe you and your husband both disengaged emotionally because it was safer. You learned not to care in order to protect yourself from further hurt and disappointment. But what you may not have realized is that stifling your feelings not only harms your marriage, it impairs your emotional health as well. When you stop letting yourself feel pain, you also block your ability to feel deep joy and other positive emotions, including love and affection for your spouse.

In order to reengage emotionally, you must be willing to care again, to be vulnerable and risk pain and rejection. In order to do this, be sure you have fully forgiven your husband for past offenses. You must begin with a clean slate, and then make a conscious decision to reopen your heart.

Renegotiate your relationship. Every relationship has invisible terms that have to do with our expectations. In marriage we have jointly, often wordlessly, agreed on the way things will be, the way they will work. Molly says, "Our terms looked like this: We will go our separate ways in the evening. We will not talk about the relationship unless it's to make negative comments. We don't let each other see our pain or tears. We have an unspoken agreement that we're staying together for the kids' sake. We are expected to be civil. I'm expected to clean house. John is expected to bring home the bacon."

If your husband is willing, ask for his input about what changes to negotiate. Set up a meeting and take notes. Ask each other: What do we want this marriage to be? How can we take one small step toward togetherness? What routines or patterns can we purposely change in order to create more intimacy or unity between us?

If your husband is unwilling to talk or renegotiate, you can renegotiate your part by yourself. Decide what you want to change. Write it down. Pray over it. If you begin to implement changes, it will dramatically affect the relationship. When one partner changes his or her patterns, the other partner always reacts. For example, if you stop yelling at him when you argue, you'll be changing the usual dynamics and he won't be able to yell back if that's his usual response.

Try to have new conversations. Many couples fall into a conversation rut. Molly says, "I think one reason John and I didn't talk anymore is that we had a repertoire of exactly five conversations which we had over and over. We talked about the kids and their problems. We talked about John's latest peeves with a peer at his work. We talked about money. We often talked about how we both really should have been exercising more and needed to lose weight. Sometimes it struck me as funny, and I'd tell John we should just make tapes of our five conversations and play them back instead of saying the same things all over again."

It may sound hokey and feel artificial, but it is crucial for you to find new topics for discussion. The trick is to find things that you both are interested in. Try to ask questions that probe the other's personality. Go see an unusual movie together and talk about it. Ask your husband something ridiculous, like "What would you do if you won the lottery?" At first such conversation might seem forced, but often the discussion will gradually lead into a genuine exploration of a topic.

Find a way to have fun together. Or at least find a way to both be enjoying yourselves in the same vicinity. The path back to a marriage with feeling is the path of friendship. And friendships are formed when two people have fun together. If your husband is at all amenable, try to find a new activity you both might enjoy. Join a volleyball league. Take up fishing together. If he doesn't want to try something new, see if he might be willing to involve you in something he already enjoys. In fact, it might be as small as deciding to run two miles together every day after dinner instead of watching the local news. Making one small change like this can be the catalyst to a changed life and marriage.

Get nostalgic. One way to revive the feelings of love that you experienced early on in marriage is to revisit those times. Pull out old scrapbooks. Find that letter he wrote you. Spend time reminiscing about how you fell in love. What did you feel? How did you see your husband? What was it about him that really attracted you to him?

Invite your husband to join you by asking him a question like, "Can you remember our first three dates?" A long conversation about the early days can do wonders to rekindle the desire to feel love again.

Dream a new dream. One of the most painful things about a not-so-perfect marriage is the death of a dream. You may not even realize that you had one, but you did. You pictured how your marriage would be. And it wasn't this. Maybe you thought you were marrying a man with money and a future full of promise, but now he's unemployed and you're miles from the white picket fence.

Your husband had a dream too. And guess what? You're probably not it either. Remember, he's likely just as disappointed and disillusioned as you are.

Sometimes when a dream dies, we need to consciously acknowledge its death, have a cry, and let it go. Only then can we begin to dream a new dream, much less embrace it.

The Bible tells us, "Where there is no vision, the people perish" (Proverbs 29:18, KJV). It could also be said that "where there is no dream, the people divorce." One of the best ways to improve your marriage is to begin to dream dreams with your husband.

And if he's content to be stuck where he is and isn't willing to dream with you, dream on your own and pray that God will resurrect the desire to dream in his heart. As much as possible, share with him your own thoughts and hopes for the future. When your husband sees that you're excited, he just might catch the dream bug himself.

Whether you dream together or alone, it's important to get outrageous. Throw out all the preconceived notions and limitations, like "We can't move to another town" or "I make too much money at this job to quit." Sometimes making a big change—moving out of the city to a small town or going back to graduate school—can reenergize a marriage.

Do you believe God wants to do a new thing in your lives? Pray for a vision of a different future. Seek Him and His power with all your heart for your marriage. If you haven't ever fasted and prayed, try it. Now!

Remember, God loves your marriage even when you can't feel love for each other. God has plans for the two of you to become something wonderful together even when you can't see it. And God will never ever give up on your marriage even when you want to.

Dear God,

When I feel no hope for my marriage, when love feels like it's died, remind me of what's true: There is always hope because of Your resurrection power at work. Keep teaching the truth of the cliché: Love is not something I feel, but something I do. Please restore in both of us a desire for change and growth. Lead us to the path that will bring healing and fresh starts. I choose to believe that You can save this marriage. Only help me to do my part. Amen.

VOICES: KIM'S STORY

Kim and Nick were both previously divorced and desired to make their second marriage succeed. Kim says the healing process has been more painful than she imagined, but it's worth all the hard work to be where they are today.

Nick and I have been married thirteen years. There were times during the first half of our marriage when I didn't think we were going to make it.

We didn't have a clue about how to have a good marriage. We fought about everything—how to discipline the kids, who should make decisions, how we should spend money, who should do particular household chores, which family we should visit the next weekend. Neither one of us wanted to sacrifice anything, and we both stubbornly insisted on having our own way. Our arguments were punctuated by long silences. We didn't have any tools to help us talk to each other about what we were feeling, to hear each other's hearts. Our immaturity kept us living separately within our marriage.

Finally, in desperation, I started seeing a counselor. I told Nick that if he was at all interested in our marriage, that we *both* needed counseling. He agreed and eventually joined me. It didn't take long before we realized we had to reinvent our marriage. We had to learn to relate in radically different ways instead of destroying our marriage with angry insults, self-righteousness, and self-centered attitudes.

One of the first things we did was talk about our childhoods and the expectations that each of us had brought into the marriage. This was very significant for me. Both of my parents were strong, independent individuals, and so am I. Of course, I expected Nick to be the strong one, the leader in our marriage. I wanted him to engage in life, not to be so passive. I kept demanding that he be a certain way. Both in my words and actions, I told him, "This is what you should be. This is who God wants you to be." I told Nick what books to read, what clothes to wear, what he should and should not say, and how he should act. I was so busy talking that neither of us could hear God's voice. Nick felt overwhelmed and emasculated while I felt frustrated and angry.

I also began to see that my need to control Nick came out of my own inadequacies and hurts. I needed healing if I was going to change the way I related to him and others. And I needed to take my hands off of Nick, so that God could heal him. Once I got out of the way, Nick could hear what the Lord was saying to him.

Over time I stopped looking to Nick to fill all my needs and started finding my security in the Lord. I started working on changing myself—and I quit trying to change Nick.

I asked God to become my source of security and meditated on verses that defined who I am in Christ. I prayed that He would show me my heart, what areas needed His healing touch. Slowly He began to peel away my layers of hurt like an onion. I became aware of childhood issues that needed healing and forgiveness.

Nick and I found spiritual mentors, a mature Christian couple who encouraged, supported, and prayed for us and our marriage. They helped keep us accountable and gave us wise advice about how to approach issues.

I'm amazed at how different our marriage is today. Only a few years ago, I didn't trust Nick. I didn't confide in him. I didn't enjoy being with him. Frankly, I didn't even like him. When a friend suggested I write down ten things I liked about my husband, I couldn't even write one—and Nick's a good guy!

But God has brought us a long way since that day. Now I can write pages about what I like about my husband. I consider him my friend, confidant, and lover. Someone I trust.

Our counselor used to pray that God would give Nick and me more from our marriage. We would say, "Oh, no, not the More prayer!" We thought that meant more changes, more pain. What it has meant, though, is more blessing, more freedom, more love.

four

"About My Husband, Lord..."

Instead of fretting and worrying about the problems in your marriage, pray about them. Gather up your concerns and requests for yourself and your husband and leave the whole load at the feet of Jesus. Pray with a thankful heart, knowing God promises to hear and answer you. Then Christ Himself will give you a peace so powerful and steady that it defies explanation.

A PARAPHRASE OF PHIIPPIANS 4:6

pecial courage is required when you're in a difficult marriage and trying to pray for your husband. It can be lonely and frustrating. You don't see the changes in him you'd hoped for. Sometimes you're tempted to throw up your hands, quit praying for improvement in your marriage, and instead beg God to simply end it.

Maybe you are so sick of praying for your husband that when you saw this chapter title, you thought: *Whenever I pray for my husband nothing happens. All I feel is frustrated, angry, and confused. I'm beginning to wonder why I pray at all! I certainly don't feel like it!*

First, remember that we're never told to pray because we feel like it. We are told to pray fervently—passionately, with faith and force-fulness. Prayer is not based on feelings. Prayer is an act of obedience to a loving God who wants to talk to you about what concerns you.

When we accept God's invitation to a praying ministry in our marriage, we have a very real advantage over the forces that war against our marriage each day. Repeatedly and gently we're reminded of God's loving commitment to us. We receive the peace and joy He has promised. We discover new insights into old problems, and often we're surprised to discover how much our *own* lives change.

What's more, even if we don't see the immediate impact of our prayers, God promises that our prayers are effective.

As the psalmist says, "[He] has not rejected my prayer!" (Psalm 66:20). As amazing as it sounds, God has promised to respond to our petitions.

"Which of you, if his son asks for bread, will give him a stone?" Jesus asked. "If you, then, though you are evil, know how to give good gifts to your children, how much more will your Father in heaven give good gifts to those who ask him" (Matthew 7:9, 11).

Jesus promised that every prayer of a God-seeking person would be answered. "Everyone who asks receives," He said (Matthew 7:8). Always.

But that doesn't mean that we get what we ask for. The answer to our prayer—which may at first appear to be no answer—might really be yes or no, direct or indirect, immediate or deferred. The change we seek outside ourselves—"Please help Mike to stop complaining"—becomes a prayer for change within—"Lord, teach me how to listen to my husband so that he feels genuinely heard."

Sometimes we must continue to pray, even though it's the last thing we feel like doing, even though God's answers on deeply felt issues remain wrapped in mystery.

But while it's true that our feelings don't matter in prayer, our motives do. How can our motives be pure if, when we pray for our husbands, we feel more angry and distraught than compassionate and loving?

Your motive has to do with what you hope your prayer will accomplish, the reason you're praying in the first place, and the attitude you bring. Prayer mentors Warren and Ruth Myers write:

> Prayer is not a way of getting what we want, but the way to become what God wants us to be.
>
> ANONYMOUS

Especially when we're asking God to overcome (another person's) negative qualities, we must be on guard against the sin of a critical, proud spirit cloaked in prayer. When we're concerned about a person's negative qualities, it helps to think through to the corresponding positive qualities we hope for, and pray for those. We personally find it easier to have faith for the positives than against the negatives."[1]

How can you check your motives in praying for your husband? One way is to take a "love inventory" based on Paul's well-known hymn to true love, 1 Corinthians 13:4–8. For example:

The prayer of love is patient: Am I praying for my husband with a tolerant, persevering, and realistic attitude (the kind of attitude I need in return on a regular basis)?

The prayer of love is kind: Am I praying for my husband with a determination to understand him, to listen, to believe the best about him, to forgive him?

The prayer of love is not self-seeking: What's at stake here—my rights, my preferences, my way? Have I resolutely tried to see the big picture and "pray with the mind of Christ"?

The prayer of love is not boastful or proud: In every request for my husband, do I keep my own ever-present failings in mind? Are my words and tone in prayer genuinely humble?

The prayer of love believes and hopes and endures: Do I pray with all the crazy passion and boundless enthusiasm I felt at our wedding? Do I pray, too, with all the faith and trust that God has been nourishing in me in the years since?[2]

Our attitude makes a difference when we are praying for our husbands. Without love, all a wife's well-intentioned petitions are just noise (1 Corinthians 13:1). Without outward behavior to match an inward attitude of mutual respect and consideration, our pious requests won't get past the ceiling (1 Peter 3:7).

Remember, on your journey of prayer you never pray alone. You are actually joining with Christ in His greatest work. He, too, stands before the Father interceding for you and your marriage (Romans 8:34). And He gives us His Spirit to help us as we pray (Romans 8:26–27).

When you think about it, the opportunity to pray for your husband is an amazing invitation from the One who loves him most.

Yes, prayer takes patience, discipline, and at times it feels costly. But it is the only sure way to know that we are releasing God's power into our marriage and our own lives.

Dear Lord,
Today I pray for breakthroughs in my ability and
commitment to pray for my husband. How easily I
forget that this—prayer—is the most effective tool I
have! If only I would pray more and talk less. Pray
more and worry less. Pray more and manipulate
less. Power is in prayer, not in my measly efforts to
bring improvement or change. Help me to get that.
To really get that. Apart from You, I can do nothing!
Nada. Zero. Today I want to make a new
commitment, Lord, to pray for my husband fervently,
frequently, and in love. Help me to do this. You know
I can't do it without You. My promises and good
intentions are like sawdust without Your power at
work in my life. Amen.

five

What Was God Thinking?

It didn't take God long to see that Adam was in need
of help, a partner, someone with qualities he lacked.
So God made woman to help and to complete man.

A PARAPHRASE OF GENESIS 2:18

When Eve first laid eyes on Adam, she asked God a question that women have been asking ever since: "Is that your final answer?"

Genesis tells us that God created Adam and Eve in different ways, at different times, for different purposes, and to be simply, beautifully different!

But that wasn't the end of the miracle. Then He brought them to each other and said, "The two shall become one...."

Sometimes you wonder what He was thinking! How can two so very different people ever become one? Particularly when the typical woman needs and wants a relationship more than her husband does. Most men don't even like the word *relationship*, aren't sure what it means, and don't know why they should work at one. Humorist Dave Barry says the sum total of the average guy's thinking on relationships is, "Huh?"

You want to cuddle; he wants to scratch. You want a soul mate; he wants dinner. You want to talk about feelings; he doesn't want to talk at all (probably because what he wants to talk about is why his favorite sports team is in a slump, and he knows you don't have any thoughts on that). You want him to take you to a nice restaurant; he wants you to lead him by his belt loops into the bedroom. You want him to care about how his words and actions injure you; he wants you to care enough to cut him some slack and please, just this once, don't bring it up.

With all these differences, the distance between you and your husband may feel like the Grand Canyon. We have to work so hard just to understand each other, don't we? And from there to appreciate and respect each other. And from there to express love and support for each other in a way that will feel like love and support to our significant opposite. Only then do the two of us even come close to being one. If your marriage is already under stress, getting across this Grand Canyon to oneness can seem like a lifelong impossibility.

Let's face it, every Eve's biggest problem always seems to be her Adam. You probably have a lot of your own Why-does-he-have-to-act-like-such-a-man? stories and insights. But today we should do the more difficult—and much more useful—thing, and look for ways to make our differences work for the good of our marriage instead of to its detriment.

Is there any promise for your marriage that is hidden among the confounding, annoying, unfixable differences you have with your husband?

Start by asking yourself three canyon-jumping questions:

How can I use our differences to bless him? Perhaps it's the touches of thoughtfulness and beauty you bring to the house or to a meal. Perhaps it's your ability to sense what your kids need to talk about today or what you need to be planning ahead about regarding your future.

Think, too, about the specific differences that attracted him to you in the first place. You are still the person he fell in love with. Ask yourself what aspects of your personality or appearance or circumstances were most appealing to him, and bless him with an expression of that same quality today.

Marisa remembers how Todd, who tends to be serious, used to always comment on her sense of humor. But with two kids under age four, she'd almost forgotten to look for the humor in life. "These days," she says, "I try to think about my trials during the day with the kids, and sometimes, when Todd comes home, it's comedy night at the Anderson house. He loves it when I'm funny and happy."

How could I say to my husband, "I'm so glad you're a man"? "Your husband is not going to be like your college roommate," writes Dr. Kevin Leman in his book, *Making Sense of the Men in Your Life*. "If you try to turn your husband into your lifelong best girlfriend, you'll be forever frustrated."[1]

Sometimes the problem is just that simple. Rather than accepting our gender differences, we keep hoping to "nurture his feminine side" or get him interested in doing the kinds of things we used to do with girlfriends. Instead, try to be intentional about having plenty of women friends in your life who meet the relationship or recreational needs that your husband can't or won't. Let him off the hook, and then look for ways to tell him you're *glad* he's a man. Encourage his male hobbies. Thank him for doing things around the house or yard that you consider a man's job.

Or try Rhoda's tactic. She says, "I keep trying to make relationship happen in Terry's language. For him that would be listening attentively to his (same old!) anxieties about work. Or treating him with respect in public. Or maybe making a veggie and chip tray for him when he settles in for his second ball game of the evening on TV. Before he turns out the light at night, I tell him, 'It's so great to be married....'"

What is one area of conflict where I could choose to accept— even celebrate—our differences? Maybe for you the greatest arena of trouble has to do with a difference in communication styles. Or maybe it's disagreements about how you spend money or how the two of you spend your time.

After Blaire had been married to Isaiah about a year, they began to have arguments about how they spent their evenings. "I like to be quiet at night, reading, taking walks and talking," she explains. "Isaiah likes to watch TV or go out to a movie. He doesn't want to have to think or talk. Then, a few months ago we had this great idea. We agreed to have an 'Isaiah night' and a 'Blaire night' once a week. He gets to pick a night when he wants me curled up watching TV with him or going to a movie. I get to pick one night when we will snuggle to quiet music or take a walk. It's been so great!"

One of the most powerful marriage restorers is the simple strategy of thanking God for your conflicts as an act of faith, believing that even though you don't see any positives now, you can trust in His goodness and wisdom enough to know that He is always working for your good (Romans 8:28).

Today is a good day to trust in God's amazing plan for man and wife and do our best to honor our other half. After all, fifty percent of the human race thinks that a woman's ways are as strange as fish climbing trees, anyway.

That's enough to keep any girl humble.

Lord and Maker,
Thank You for making us male and female. Help me
to make the most of Your plan. Show me how to
understand what it's like to be a man (within limits, I
mean!). Help me work at complementing my
husband instead of competing with him or resisting
him. Work miracles in that gap that seems to always
lie between us. Make something beautiful out of what
feels like something irreconcilable. In Your name I
pray. Amen.

When Your Bootstraps Break

*How terrible it is for a wife in a difficult marriage
who has no one to turn to for support and help! By
ourselves, we are easily overpowered by weakness
and temptation. But when we are accountable to a
friend who is fighting with us for our marriages, we
can stand firm even when we have no strength left.*

A PARAPHRASE OF ECCLESIASTES 4:9–10, 12

For many years, I didn't want anyone to know about my marriage problems. I felt too ashamed to talk about the arguments that sometimes escalated into shouting matches. So I presented a happy face to the outside world and determined to act stronger than I felt. On some level I knew I couldn't handle our problems alone, but I didn't know how to let go and seek the support I needed.

Maybe you've been there too. Why is it so hard to ask for help?

Often a combination of pride, humiliation, or shame keep us isolated. It doesn't help that our culture applauds rugged individualism and independence. We commend those who are strong and self-reliant, who seem to pull themselves up by their bootstraps, no matter what. Sometimes we label as inferior and weak or lacking in character those who seek out help. As a result, our circumstances hammer some of us before we finally admit defeat (a positive step!) and reach out for help.

After Randy and I had been married for twelve years, we moved to a new community. By this time, I was well aware of Randy's drinking problems. I looked forward to a new start, reasoning that if Randy felt less pressure with his new job, he'd be less likely to drink. But we hadn't even unpacked all the boxes when the nightmare began again. Randy came home late. He'd been drinking. Finally one night I didn't bother to confront and accuse him. All I could think of was getting out, getting help. You could say my proverbial bootstraps had finally broken.

I ran to my neighbor's house. I'd only met her once. "Nancy, I'm sorry to bother you. Randy and I are having problems."

Nancy didn't ask questions. She went to her closet and pulled out a warm comforter and pillow. She made a bed for me on the couch and sat with me during that long night, listening to my pain. Nancy became a lifeline, always offering hope and encouragement. I have no doubt that God allowed us to find a home next to Nancy's. He knew I would need her prayers, comfort, unconditional acceptance and love.

Nancy never gave pat answers or sermonized about what I ought to do. She never shamed me or questioned why I was putting up with my husband's behavior. She loved me right where I was, in a way that allowed me to take more steps toward finding support. She prayed for Randy and me and held on to hope—even when I could not.

I am grateful for the people like Nancy in my life. No one is strong enough to face her nightmares alone. God designed us to need each other. Not to say that our marital problems will disappear when we ask for help. They don't. Nor is there a magic formula or ten-point plan to fix what's wrong in our relationships. But a good friend can help us by affirming or challenging our perspective, by reminding us of what we've learned and how we've grown, by listening to us and loving us, and by praying with us about the challenges we face.

Here are some guidelines about asking for help:

Ask God for discernment in seeking help, whether it is from a caring friend or neighbor or a compassionate counselor. Sometimes finding the right sources of support is a matter of trial and error, but God can give you wisdom. Ask for recommendations for counselors and support groups. Churches often sponsor various support groups that you can visit. Try one several times before making a decision about whether it is right for you.

Be careful to choose wisely. Not everyone provides the kind of support that is truly helpful—even pastors and Christian counselors. Avoid those who want to fix you and your marriage, who always have foolproof answers, or who treat you with condescension. You'll also want to steer clear of people who can't keep confidences.

Pray about how to talk with your friends about your husband. It's tempting to bad-mouth our husbands when we're unhappy in our marriages. To recount every wrong or injustice we have suffered. Don't fall into this trap.

Proverbs 10:32 says: "The lips of the righteous know what is fitting." With God's help you can discuss your feelings in an honest way but still honor your husband. A rare friend is one who can hold these confidences and become a partner with you in prayer.

Today, remember that God sees you where you are. Scripture often talks about people who cried out for the Lord's help, and He faithfully helped them. He wants you to get the support you need, and He cares about even the smallest details (like putting a compassionate neighbor and friend in our paths).

Dear God,
Help me trust You when I feel like my life is falling
apart. When I'm afraid to ask for help, give me
courage to see who You have brought across my path.
Help me overcome my pride, my fear of humiliation
or shame. I believe Your Word is true. You will
provide a way for me and my family. We are not
alone. Amen.

seven

What About Our Children?

I know whom I have believed, and am convinced that
he is able to guard what I have entrusted to him for
that day.

2 TIMOTHY 1:12

"I don't know which house to go to," wailed five-year-old Jamie, her blue eyes pleading with her parents. Mark and Sherrie were contemplating divorce and had recently separated. Jamie spent half of each week with her mom, the other with her dad at his apartment. Inconsolable, Jamie clung to her worn, stuffed teddy bear while sucking on her pacifier. Her parents felt torn with grief and guilt.

According to *Time* magazine, more than one million children per year join the ranks of America's children of divorce.[1]

The prevailing view for the past three decades has been that divorce is no big deal for kids. Sure it's tough at first. It's hard on the whole family. But kids are resilient. They get over it. Or so everyone thought.

Judith Wallerstein, a clinical psychologist who began researching effects of divorce on children in the late sixties, presents a different, more disturbing outcome in her book, *The Unexpected Legacy of Divorce,* as excerpted from *Time* magazine,

Children take a long time to get over divorce. Indeed, its most harmful and profound effects tend to show up as children reach maturity and struggle to form their own adult relationships. Parents who divorce may think of their decision to end the marriage as wise, courageous, and the best remedy for their unhappiness—indeed it may be so—but for the child, divorce carries one meaning: the parents have failed at one of the central tasks of adulthood. This failure shapes the child's inner template of self and family. If they failed, I can fail, too. And if, as happens so frequently, the child observes more failed relationships in the years after divorce, the conclusion is simple. I have never seen a man and a woman together on the same beam. Failure is inevitable.[2]

What about our children? Will they be okay in a not-so-perfect marriage, or are they better off if their parents end their marriage? Kathy, who was divorced when her children were eight and ten, recalled a conversation with her now-grown son. He said, "I thought we were the Cleavers. I thought everything was fine. Then one day Dad said he was leaving. I used to hear you crying at night. I hid under my pillow so I couldn't hear you cry." Kathy wonders how to measure the impact of divorce on her son and daughter.

Linda J. Waite and Maggie Gallagher write in their book, *The Case for Marriage: Why Married People Are Happier, Healthier, and Better off Financially:*

While staying together for the sake of the children was once the norm, today's Americans are more likely to tell an unhappy couple that they should divorce—even for the sake of the children. Adults may prefer to be joyously in love, but children don't care whether parents zoom to heights of romantic ecstasy or not. Your children don't care whether your marriage feels dead or alive, empty or full. As long as Mom and Dad don't fight too much, they thrive under the love, attention, and resources two married parents provide.[3]

Therein lies the difficulty: determining when a marriage has reached the point of no return, when it is more harmful to stay rather than leave. According to recent research, in almost every situation it is better for the children when parents stay together. The one exception is abusive relationships. (See appendix, questions 1 and 3). However, contrary to what many believe, less than one-third of all divorces end angry, high-conflict marriages.

As parents, as moms, we need to consider the risks for our children when we consider divorce an option. As Christians we have the advantage of God's unlimited resources and wisdom. In prayer we can determine what is best for our children and for us. God is able to do immeasurably more than what we could ever imagine. He can renew our love for our husbands and bring healing, reconciliation, and restoration of our relationships. And even if our marriages never become what we desire, God can change our hearts so we experience contentment, peace, even joy. It's possible!

Cindy, mother of three, stated, "If my husband and I had divorced, sure, our kids would probably have lived without as much fighting. But they wouldn't have seen that even though we fight and basically don't like each other at times, we have worked through problems and come out on the other side as friends."

Dennis Rainey asks this difficult question in his book, *One Home at a Time,* "Will we act courageously on behalf of the next generation and do what God expects of us in our own families to bring about change one home at a time?"[4]

What or how much should I tell our children about their father's failings and our resulting problems?

We have an opportunity to pass on a rich heritage to our children. We can model God's love, forgiveness, His plan for marriage and commitment to our spouses. What greater gift can we give them?

At my parents' fiftieth anniversary celebration, I couldn't help but reminisce. Mom and Dad didn't always get along. They disagreed. They argued. But the fact is, they loved each other and they loved us kids. They sacrificed their own happiness at times for us. They hung in there and did their best, which was a lot. I pray Randy and I will have the privilege of passing their legacy on to our children.

You may feel guilty and somehow responsible for your husband's failings. *Or* you may feel innocent and misunderstood. If you feel guilty, you may want your children to understand the roots of the problem in order to shift, or at least equalize, the weight of guilt. If you feel innocent, you may want your children to know more in order to guarantee their image of you as a loving parent, a parent who would never let them down.

Either way, you lose if you tell the children everything. Either way, in regard to how much your children should know, the answer is the same—not much. While you don't want your children to grow up naive or spiritually unaware, your charge is to offer them a soft place to fall—in you. A place where they can be at home, a place where trust is proven. Your priorities should include preserving the innocence of your children—not because ignorance is bliss, but because you want them to emerge as healthy as possible.

That said, in many situations, you *will* need to talk with your children about what is happening. When there is overt evidence of something drastically amiss, you shouldn't ignore it or act as if nothing is going on. If your husband is an alcoholic, for example, rather than deny what is obvious, you should explain that Daddy has a problem with drinking too much. Children are very intuitive, and if they sense trouble and feel lied to or kept in the dark, this may increase their insecurity.

When you do talk to your children about troubles related to your marriage or your husband, keep these guidelines in mind:

Assess what they need to know. Let their questions guide you and keep your answers appropriate to their age level. Keep in mind that often children's most vital questions will be disguised as pain, not articulated in words. They want to know, but they don't want to know. Your finest answers will be clothed in comfort, perhaps with little commentary.

Focus on what benefits them, not you. Often a child needs only a short, simple explanation rather than a long, emotionally charged discussion.

Never aim to lessen their love or respect for their father. When you shame the parent, you shame the child. If you cast their father in a negative light, the shadow of that shame will fall over the spirit of your children. Offering the toxic drink of direct truth to kids is unfair. Instead of thinking Dad is troubled or bad, a child thinks, *I am bad*.

Focus on the positive. Tell your children:

- that both you and their father love them and want them to have the best.
- how proud you are of them, how often you pray for them, how clearly you see they have what it takes to get through the difficult times in life.
- that you see them maturing and growing more loving.

- that you've learned that hard times are God's way of drawing us closer to Himself.
- that someday you'll tell them more, when the time is appropriate and if they ask.

Gather your children around you often; create warm, cozy moments—in snatches here and there. Work on reestablishing the feeling of family, even when their father does not participate. Remember, your children are also listening to everything you *don't* say.

> *Dear God,*
> *I'm thankful You are there to give me wisdom when I*
> *need it. I worry about our kids. I wonder if they'll be*
> *okay, being raised with parents who don't get along.*
> *Sometimes I feel like a failure as a parent. I've been*
> *too focused on our marriage and on my husband.*
> *Forgive me, Lord. Help me stay strong in my*
> *commitments as wife and mother. My heart's desire is*
> *to give our children the heritage of a family*
> *committed to staying together and finding healing in*
> *the process. With Your help, we can be one more*
> *home that makes a difference for our children, our*
> *community, and our country. Amen.*

eight

The Mercy Blanket

Above all, have a fervent love for your husband.
When you come upon some unsightly weakness or
sin of his, don't expose it to others or further shame
him. Instead, gently cover his sins with a blanket of
love, protecting them from view and forgiving him
from your heart.

A PARAPHRASE OF 1 PETER 4:8

As a wife, you are in a position to see all of your husband's
flaws. You see everything—his weaknesses and strengths,
his oddities and embarrassing habits. If your husband has hurt you
or disappointed you, you'll be tempted to blame his failings for
your unhappiness. And if his weaknesses have caused you pain,
you may be tempted to punish him.

And hurt him you could! You know things about your husband
that no one else knows: his struggle with pornography, his
tendency to spend more than he earns, the fact that he lies and
embellishes things to make himself look good to your friends, his
frustration over impotence…. Such intimate knowledge about
another person invites compassion and grace—or betrayal and
regret. If you betray your husband's secrets, you exploit your intimate knowledge of him and hurt him deeply.

Keep a secret and it is

yours; tell it to God

and it's prayer;

tell it to people

and it's gossip.

UNKNOWN

What are some ways that women exploit their husband's vulnerabilities?

In the form of prayer requests. You tell your friend Kasha that your husband Steve is terrible with money, and that he's going to have to declare bankruptcy on his business. You ask her to pray for him. But you spend ten minutes describing how Steve drives you crazy. Kasha promises not to tell her husband Mark about the bankruptcy. She consoles you and validates you. She agrees with your opinion that it's Steve's own fault he failed. "If he would have listened to you..." You get the picture.

There's nothing wrong with sharing some of your marriage problems with a close friend you can trust. But sometimes there is a fine line between honestly seeking support—and deliberately exploiting your husband's weaknesses or faults to gain sympathy or promote some ulterior agenda.

So how can you tell the difference?

If you are going to reveal something about your husband, first ask yourself:

- What is my motive? Am I looking for sympathy and someone to further arm me for battle and make me feel right?
- What would my husband feel about my sharing this?
- What does my gut, my spiritual barometer, tell me?

By poking fun of him in public. Your husband tells you he's sure his office party you're about to attend together is casual, and he insists on wearing a polo shirt. When you arrive at the gathering, he's the only man not wearing a tie. Throughout the evening you make a point of his blunder with jokes like, "Jack probably wouldn't wear a suit to his own funeral!"

So often what is humorous to us can be hurtful to our husbands. And though the offense may seem small to us, because it is a betrayal, it chips away at your husband's ability to trust you with his heart and with matters of greater importance.

The opposite of publicly poking at our guys is to praise them to others. Think about how wonderful it makes you feel when your husband talks you up in public. "Jenny here is amazing," he says, putting his arm around your shoulders. "You should see what she did with our old kitchen. Now it looks like Martha Stewart lives there!" Determine how you could build him up this same way.

In fact, if you tend to speak before you think, before going to any social functions with your husband, consider what weaknesses or recent foibles of his you might let slip. For example, let's say he's still not gotten around to fixing your teenage son's beat-up car, and it's been bugging you all week. You can just hear yourself saying, "I don't think Bill will get to it until our yard is declared a wrecking yard!" Instead, have a private smile and then determine *not to say a word* about whatever it is. Better yet, try to think of three positive things you'll mention in others' hearing about your husband's good qualities or accomplishments.

By throwing his failures and mistakes back in his face in the heat of an argument. When we're engaged in a verbal battle and trying to make a point, it's only natural that we reach for evidence to back it up. "There was this time…." and "Remember when you…?" However, using past mistakes to prove present culpability usually hurts and proves ineffective. The more past mistakes you list, the higher his wall of defensiveness builds. Pretty soon you've reopened old wounds, wounds from offenses already forgiven that should be filed in a box in your heart marked "Covered by the Blood."

The same goes for attacking your husband's areas of vulnerability. You know exactly where it will hurt most: "If you hadn't lost that job in Chicago, we wouldn't be having this argument about finances right now!" This is like saying, "I want to stab you in that place where I know the knife will go deepest." Can you think of several areas of past sin or failure where you know your husband is especially vulnerable to hurtful remarks? Will you decide that you will do everything in your power to build him up in those areas rather than tear him down?

The flip side of betrayal is to cover a multitude of sins with love (1 Peter 4:8). Your husband's weaknesses or failures offer you an amazing, powerful opportunity to show him love and mercy. It's as if you have come upon a wound, an ugly protrusion. (That's what seeing our mate's sins can feel like!) But love, rather than screaming for others to come look, gently lays a blanket of mercy over our mate, protecting him and forgiving what has been revealed.

> *Dear Lord,*
> *I want to show my husband mercy and protection rather than exploit his secret failings. Show me how to do that in a very practical way each day. Thank You that You not only cover over our sins with Your blood, but You are also able to completely forgive them! May I practice that same kind of forgiveness with my husband. The kind that says: "I won't use this against you. I forgive you. I love you." Amen.*

nine

Martyrs Anonymous

*Search my soul, O God, until you know my heart
and all its secrets. Test my anxious thoughts and
measure the merits of my sadness; show me anything
in my marriage that is offensive to you, and lead me
in the way of those who overcome.*

A PARAPHRASE OF PSALM 139:23–24

'm sure I'm a charter member of Martyrs Anonymous. For years anyone who talked to me about our marriage could almost hear violins playing in the background. *Poor, brave little woman. How can he treat such a sweet wife that way?*

Once, after recounting my quiet suffering in the face of Randy's latest grievous sins against me, an empathetic counselor remarked, "You should win the Joan of Arc award of the year!" In my naiveté I considered that a compliment.

Now I can look back and see the humor in his statement. But it took a long time for me to realize that I found my identity in being a martyr.

The word *martyr is* used to refer to someone who has sacrificed his or her life for a great or religious cause. Christian history is full of martyrs. But today we often use the word in a negative sense to refer to someone who seems to enjoy or take pride in a pattern of suffering and sacrifice. When you play the martyr with your husband, you choose the role of victim—and then pump it for all it's worth. The gain? Sympathy. An appearance of being noble. And a familiar, comfortable routine.

The loss? When you grow comfortable in a martyr role, your husband feels all the more comfortable in the worn-out role of Bad Guy. Because you see yourself as a victim rather than a victor, instead of seeking solutions and change, you resign yourself to suffering. As a result, you and your marriage stay stuck in the mud.

How can you know if you are playing the victim or martyr role? Try asking yourself these questions:

- Do you frequently make casual comments to friends and acquaintances about how lucky other wives are or how unfortunate you are?
- Do you automatically reach for the phone immediately after a marital conflict so you can receive sympathy and get confirmation that you're right?
- Are you convinced that you have no power outside of prayer to change things in your marriage?
- Has being a wife in a difficult marriage become important to your sense of identity? In other words, is your friend Jodie the hilarious friend everyone wants at their party, while you're that woman in the difficult marriage that everyone likes and feels so sorry for?
- Do you gain comfort from comparisons between your perseverance and commitment and your husband's failings and disappointing behavior?
- Do you often cloak a plea for sympathy in a request for prayer?
- Do you feel resistant or offended when someone suggests you might have a role in your marriage problems?
- Do you use crying or displays of grief to punish your husband with guilt?

All of us have probably done some of these things. But if this is a problem area for you, by now you should have plenty of red lights flashing.

Once you realize you've been stuck playing a martyr role, it takes time to change. You might want to pursue the topic with a counselor. But you can also set about imposing some changes on yourself:

Ask yourself: Is there some reason I need or want to feel like the victim? When I asked myself this question, I knew instinctively that the answer was yes. Just the thought of someone taking away my right to be hurt and a victim felt threatening. After much soul searching, I realized that I was trying to punish Randy with my suffering and tears. If he was going to disappoint me, I was going to make him miserable with guilt, or at least uncomfortable in front of the world.

In one sense, I was successful. Our roles were hard to miss: Randy the irresponsible one and Deb the loving, nobly persevering wife.

But the results were not what I'd hoped for. Instead of seeing the contrast between us and feeling shamed or sorry, Randy had become immune to feeling guilt about my suffering. As for me, I'd become so expectant of Randy letting me down that I practically invited him to, and he was happy to oblige me.

Identify your triggers. Every unhealthy pattern between two people has situational and emotional triggers. Whenever Randy came home drunk again, I would play the victim. Maybe you play the martyr whenever your husband loses his temper and yells. Think about the conflicts you have again and again, and then look at what triggers you to play the martyr.

Decide beforehand on a fresh way of coping with trigger situations. Once you identify the triggers, you can choose to respond differently. For example, let's say you tend to cry and rant every time he comes home after the kids are already in bed. Purposely set about to change that pattern. Decide to refuse to let his rudeness and tardiness ruin your evening. When he comes home, tell him you're sorry he missed out on the fun time you and the kids had playing Monopoly, and then go take a bubble bath.

Take responsibility for your part in improving your marriage and yourself. Martyrs don't feel they need to change, they only need to whine, cry, and give prayer requests about how their husband needs to change. Being martyrs keeps the focus on the offenses of our husbands, not on us.

But the moment you decide you are not a victim, you will realize that you *can* change your marriage because *you* can change you. You can control how you respond to your husband's failings, what you do with your emotions. You can control what you say and even your tone of voice if you want to!

Let's face it. If you are in a difficult marriage, you have a right to feel like a martyr at times. After all, you are making sacrifices. Maybe you've had to sacrifice the romance that you longed for or your desire for a peaceful home or a godly dad for your kids. The list goes on and on.

But you are not a victim. You can lay aside self-pity and the kind of public suffering that doesn't bring about change and hope. You can refuse to use your pain to manipulate anyone, including your husband. You can say, once and for all, "I'm not a victim in this marriage. I am a victor in Christ."

Dear Lord,
Forgive me for being a martyr for the wrong cause,
for wallowing in self-pity. Help me to dramatically
change the way I see my situation. When I feel I'm
without options, remind me that I'm not. When I feel
victimized, show me how to respond in a way that is
honest and constructive. Give me grace today, Lord.
You know I need it. Thank You that through You I am
not a victim but a victor in all things. Amen

VOICES: ANNE'S STORY

Anne and Tom have been married for eight years. They have two daughters, seven and five years old. Anne says some days are better than others. She allows herself an occasional pity party, then finds a lot of reasons to be grateful for her life.

My husband, Tom, is a good man. He dutifully goes to work each day to provide for us. But when he comes home, he settles into his easy chair with the remote control and zones out. I long to talk with him, tell him about my day, ask him about his. I want to know what he thinks about all day long. But his one-word responses have taught me that I can't get anywhere. I've given up trying. Day after day it goes like this, even though I've told him that I long for greater intimacy. He says he's happy in our marriage, and he doesn't seem to even understand what I'm asking for! How long am I supposed to hang in there, hoping for some change?

Some days I just want to be angry.

Last week, after listening to me complain about my marriage, a friend suggested I listen to some praise music. "It will lift your spirits," she said. I wanted to laugh right in her face. She has no idea what it's like having an emotionally absent husband. It's hard to climb out of the depression, to refocus my energy and thoughts on what's right with my life.

But…. I know she's right.

Wallowing in self-pity doesn't help. I might not feel like praise music, but maybe I'll call a friend, go for a walk…do something I enjoy. Now there's a concept!

Have I become so consumed with what's wrong with my marriage that I've forgotten what brings me joy? I rarely notice and appreciate the broad pink and gold brushstrokes of a sunset or the intricate detail of a frosted spider web on a cool morning. Or children laughing while they wait for the school bus outside. Do I even hear my own children's laughter?

I don't want to discount my feelings—they are real. But maybe I can learn to vent how I feel without allowing my feelings to consume me. I'm learning to journal about how I feel, and that helps me keep my problems in perspective. When I get beyond self and think about what is true, noble, pure, lovely, excellent, or praiseworthy, it's impossible to be negative at the same time. I know I can't change Tom, but I don't have to sit around feeling sorry for myself. With God's help, I can change my thinking. He will meet me in my weakness and give me strength to choose a new and different way of relating to my husband.

ten

Bitter or Beautiful?

*Rejoice whenever you face trials in your marriage,
knowing that even though it hurts right now, as your
faith is tested by these troubles, you are developing
perseverance. As you persevere in love, you will grow
increasingly more mature in heart and mind, and
God's beauty will be made complete in you.*

A PARAPHRASE OF JAMES 1:2–4

Two of the most wonderful, sweet, strong women Marie knows are married to chauvinistic, bossy, unlikable men. For years she tried to fathom how these women could be so happy in spite of being married to what most people would call jerks. These are Christian men, mind you. Good providers, well respected, and even active in their churches. But they talk on and on about themselves and their accomplishments, order their wives about, don't keep themselves fit or healthy, and generally aren't much fun to be with.

The wives? According to Marie, they are not just happy, but caring and strong and deeply spiritual. Helen dresses like a million bucks and blesses hundreds of people every year with her gift for entertaining and encouragement. Tammi writes and speaks and has only positive things to say about her home life.

One day, after a sunny encounter with Helen, Marie and her

husband, Tom, started wondering aloud how such jerky guys landed such amazing women.

"Maybe that's the key," mused Tom. "Maybe they became these wonderful, caring, amazing women because their husbands forced them to make a choice. Either learn how to be broken, how to forgive, how to love a man who's not that lovable—or get bitter and ugly."

Marie and Tom had hit on the oyster principle: homely oyster plus annoying grain of sand plus the right attitude plus time equals a pearl of great beauty and value.

Sounds easy, and the lovely outcome is there for all to see, but we know that making something beautiful out of a bad relationship is anything but easy or automatic. Mean treatment brings out our own meanness. Low blows make us aim low. Long-term, emotional battery can leave us withdrawn, judgmental, angry, and drowning in bitterness. Before long our inner self has become more beastlike than beautiful.

And that's a long way from pearls.

How, then, can we allow our daily tests to turn us into something lovely, not wretched?

For starters, look at the Scripture cited at the opening of this chapter. James wrote his letter to persecuted men and women who were faced with unrelenting disrespect, daily unfairness, rejection, hatred, violence, and death. But he's bold enough to start his advice to them like this: "Consider it pure joy…."

Every woman in a challenging relationship has a lot to learn from James and those early Christians. In the words that follow, we see some reasons James says we can find joy in abysmal circumstances:

- You are gaining maturity.
- You are being changed for the better.
- You are being made complete…"perfect," in fact!

That is the picture of loveliness.

No wonder James starts his advice with the word *consider.* How we look at a crummy situation makes all the difference. We need to step back and see that God is in control, God is at work, and, best of all, He's at work on us!

But there's more to the equation. We have to cooperate with what God is doing if we want to see results. James's fellow apostle Peter gives us a little more insight on how we go about that:

> His divine power has given us everything we need for life and godliness through our knowledge of him who called us by his own glory and goodness. Through these he has given us his very great and precious promises, so that through them you may participate in the divine nature and escape the corruption in the world caused by evil desires. For this very reason, make every effort to add to your faith goodness; and to goodness, knowledge; and to knowledge, self-control; and to self-control, perseverance; and to perseverance, godliness; and to godliness, brotherly kindness; and to brotherly kindness, love. (2 Peter 1:3–7)

Notice some key phrases. God has given us "everything we need." Because of His great promises, we can supernaturally participate in the "divine nature." In other words, if we try to do this on our own or out of our strength, we will fail. But because we know that this isn't our destiny, we "make every effort" (that means we consciously work at it) to add to our faith an increasing list of qualities that, when put into action, when rubbed up against the sharp corners of a difficult marriage, will result in our souls' beautification.

Each of these character values is a positive response we can make under pressure:

Faith: Everything about your marriage looks dismal and hopeless. Your husband has fallen back into disappointing habits or your marriage feels like it's coming apart in an avalanche of angry scenes. The path toward inner ugliness is one of resignation and defeat. That road to beautiful happens when you "make every effort" to reach for faith instead.

Goodness: Synonyms for goodness are decency, integrity, and righteousness. When you make the effort to nurture goodness in a negative or hostile environment, you grow in goodness in ways not possible in situations where it's easy to do the right thing.

Knowledge: As you come up against walls of confusion or lack of information, you're faced with the choice to either give up or pursue answers and solutions. A difficult marriage provides you with a great opportunity to become an expert on men, marriage, compromise, what works and what doesn't. Remember, knowledge is power. And power in a woman is a beautiful thing.

Self-control: Will you keep your temper or let it rip? Will you say nothing when you want to say nothing that's good? If you keep tackling the challenge of self-control, you will learn to practice it in many other areas of your life as well.

Perseverance: A wife who day after day must patiently take the next step and then the next grows strong and sure of herself. This ongoing striving feels hard, like exercise, but it also nurtures an inner grace and strength that can't be manufactured in a day or even a hard year.

Godliness: Being in a difficult marriage makes us keenly aware of just how unholy we are and how much we need the Holy Spirit to help us at every moment. To be godly is to be like God. We wives must continually reach for Jesus' robes of righteousness—and then try to live in such a way that they fit.

Brotherly kindness: Synonyms for kindness include caring,

consideration, and benevolence. But true kindness is hard to develop and express if we are around someone who often isn't kind. Every time your husband is inconsiderate, selfish, or hateful to you, you have an opportunity to show him kindness. What a challenge! But what beauty is born when we make this choice. And what potential for bitterness if we don't.

Love: Love takes brotherly kindness to the next level. To love your husband is to lay down yourself and your rights for him. To love him is to want his best. To love him is to see past who he is right now to who he could become. When he is most unlovable, you get the chance to offer him the most powerful gift in the world. And in doing so, you are changed as much as he is.

Remember, the only person you have any control over is you, and you can choose how you will respond to your challenging marriage. You can choose to say: "I dare to trust that God is at work on me right now, bringing me to maturity, completeness, and a beautiful similarity to His Son. And I know that He can use this difficult marriage to make that happen."

Of course, a daring trust in how God works through trials doesn't make the trials go away. Every day we have to let go of a lot of dreams, a lot of "if only's." But as we do, we'll start to turn the unwanted, unfair, and unlikable grit of life into gems of adornment like mercy, grace, patience, and wisdom.

In God's great scheme of things, that's how truly beautiful women are not born but made.

Dear Lord,
That's what I want! I want to allow the trials I face in
my marriage to make me more and more beautiful. I
admit that so often I do the opposite. I lose sight of
what you could be fixing in me while I focus on fixing
my husband. And when I fix, I fail. And when I
fail…well, Lord, you know what I do. I get depressed
and bitter. I act like a beast! Today I pray that You
would make me more beautiful, moment by moment,
as You give me the grace to respond to my struggles
with courage and faith. Amen.

eleven

"My Name Is Pain"

*He has sent me to bind up your broken heart, to set
you free from whatever holds you or your husband
captive—addictions, anger, bitterness, pain. I came
so that you might know that God is on your side and
you are highly favored by your Father. I will war for
your sake against the enemies of your marriage. I
will comfort you when you grieve because of your
husband and respond to your emotions when he can't
or doesn't. I will bestow on you a crown of beauty in
place of the ashes that you feel your life has become.
I will give you gladness in place of sadness, and you
will rise up with hope to praise Me.*

A PARAPHRASE OF ISAIAH 61:1–3.

Carla told me about one of the toughest times in her marriage.
Her husband had moved out, the kids were not doing well,
and she was about to turn forty. One night in a word processing
class, her instructor told the students to enter a sentence of text so
they could have something to manipulate. Without thinking, Carla
typed in, "I am forty years old. My name is Pain."

Then her computer froze up. Try as she could, she couldn't
make that awful confession go away, much less follow the teacher's
string of instructions. Finally she asked a student next to her for

help. He read her screen with interest.

"Not doing too well tonight, Carla?" he asked.

"No," she said, fighting back tears. Unfortunately, the student couldn't seem to help. Soon a second classmate and the instructor were gathered around Carla's desk, trying to unjam her program and reading her two-sentence biography.

"I am forty years old. My name is Pain."

"That was the low point," Carla says now. "My dumb life stuck on that dumb computer monitor for all to see."

Yet she also looks back at that season as a precious, though excruciating, gift. "Months later I was actually able to write in my journal that I was thankful that Wade broke my heart. He never came back. But my pain forced me to relate to God in an intimate way I never knew was possible. I found out that His comfort is real. I discovered that experiencing deep pain allowed me to also experience moments of joy more keenly than ever. And maybe best of all, my pain opened up my creative spirit as I struggled to find ways to express what I was feeling in words and in art."

Do you think that the pain you feel from love can actually bring you good? Carla's story points to those unwanted but priceless gifts that the wounds of love can bring us: greater intimacy with Christ, the experience of His comfort, increased ability to feel joy, and personal and spiritual insights that help us understand ourselves better.

Of course, when we first commit ourselves to marriage, we do so (at least usually) because love seems an easy gift. But by opening ourselves to love, we also open ourselves to hurt. As John Welwood writes in *Journey of the Heart,* "A relationship that has any depth and power at all will inevitably penetrate our usual shield of defenses, exposing our most tender and sensitive spots, and leaving us feeling vulnerable—literally, 'able to be wounded.'"[1]

When our commitment to marriage exposes us to deep hurt, we face one of the most important choices of our lives—How will we react to our pain?

When we're really suffering, the rule of pain can turn into a full-blown tyranny. We get so desperate for relief that we try to find a way to anesthetize it. We make choices in the hope that we'll be distracted from, or even released from, the torrents of pain for a while. Some women run up all the credit cards or begin an affair. Some try to cover up the hurt with alcohol or some other mind-numbing technique. But in the end, these choices usually only increase the pain.

So what do you do with the pain?

The only real way out is through it. Carla says, "I remember the day I realized that I needed to just embrace the pain, be in pain. Let it hurt. And that I wouldn't die. It wouldn't kill me."

Embracing your pain might mean that when you are feeling hurt, you sit alone with it rather than running to a friend or trying to distract yourself. It might also mean that when you cry, instead of trying to stop, you let yourself go, and maybe you even yell or scream or rant at the walls or God (He can handle it!).

Something else Carla did was begin a pain journal. "I bought this little blank book and whenever I was hurting most, I wrote in it. I talked about my pain, cried out to God. Now this is a precious record of a time when God carried me through."

The best response you can have to pain is to express it to your heavenly Father. He understands your hurt and feels your sadness. Marriage is, after all, His design. It wasn't His intention that it would bring us such pain. When I'm in deep pain, I often find comfort in reading the Psalms, particularly David's. Like us, his moods swung wildly, and often his feelings of despair clouded his vision for a time. While David never wrote about the pain of a difficult marriage, he certainly wrote about many of the hurts that come from such a marriage: betrayal, deception, anger, sadness, and loneliness. David often begins by venting and ends up worshiping. When we express to God our feelings of disappointment and hurt, we, too, will find our faith bolstered.

Let's face it, when we choose to stay in a challenging marriage, we have chosen to live with a certain amount of pain for a very long time. If a marriage has deep fractures, the healing process can be very slow, painfully slow. But if we surrender our distress to our loving Lord, we can look forward to what His healing Spirit can do in our hearts and in our ministry with others, perhaps only through pain.

You might be having another of those days when you feel like your name is Pain. You might feel that your wounds of love are up there on the computer monitor of life for all to see. If so, be encouraged that God has something better in mind for you today. With your cooperation and trust, He is up to something beautiful in your life. One day it will adorn your life like a priceless gift that will bless you, touch others for good, and bring glory to God.

> *Dear Lord,*
> *Thank You that when I hurt, You promise to comfort*
> *me. How it must grieve You when instead of coming*
> *to You with my pain, I run from it or try to smother*
> *it. Today I come with my hand open, pain in my*
> *palm. I hurt. Please touch me where I hurt in a way*
> *that brings healing and hope. Please give me courage*
> *and grace to embrace my pain and to make it*
> *through to the other side. I praise You for what I*
> *know awaits me there: joy! Amen.*

twelve

Am I Devoted or a Doormat?

You can tell a wife of noble character because she has plenty of strength and dignity. When she thinks about her future, she doesn't worry or cower, but smiles with confidence. She speaks with wisdom and carefully nurtures the relationships within her family. Her children trust her and call her blessed. Her husband agrees, and he praises her wholeheartedly.

A PARAPHRASE OF PROVERBS 31:25–28

During the years when Randy was drinking a lot and our marriage was on the rocks, I often struggled with dilemmas like this one: If I laid down a rule that I would not fix Randy dinner if he stayed out drinking past 8 P.M., I felt like I wasn't being a good Christian wife. I'd think, *What about going the extra mile, thinking of others first, forgiving seventy times seven?* But when I leaned the other way, toward Christian love and sacrifice—jumping up to make him dinner when he wandered in drunk at 10 P.M.—I felt taken advantage of and disrespected.

Can you relate? Almost every Christian wife in a difficult marriage has wrestled with similar questions: How can I care for my own needs, set limits, or say no to my husband without feeling selfish, unsubmissive, or ungodly? And how can I possibly obey the Bible's radical commands to love and devote myself to my husband without becoming a doormat?

The answer is *boundaries*. It's a word we hear used a great deal in regard to our personal relationships, but what are boundaries, really?

A boundary is an invisible line that you have drawn around yourself to represent the limits or rules you've established that govern what you will do or will not do, what you will tolerate or will not tolerate, in a relationship. Some people grow up with clearly defined boundaries, while others don't have any at all or have boundaries that are rigid and excessive. Wives without boundaries need to establish some, or they risk having problems in their relationships. And wives who have rigid boundaries need to lighten up and find a healthy balance, or they, too, will have relationship problems.

"Boundary problems are usually seen as someone's inability to either say 'no' or hear 'no' from others," explains Dr. Henry Cloud, coauthor of *Boundaries*. "When we have these kinds of problems, we either allow people to walk all over us in a way that destroys respect, or we walk all over them and 'trespass' against them, destroying love in the process. True love respects each other's boundaries, saying 'no' when we need to, and respecting it when we hear it."[1]

When a wife has healthy boundaries, she's in a much stronger position to choose to selflessly love her husband from a position of strength rather than weakness. Such a wife is not a doormat, even though she may behave sacrificially.

If you struggle to understand the difference between being devoted to your husband in a godly way and being his doormat, the following guidelines might provide some insight:

Keep Scripture in context: When you look at certain Scriptures, like those in Matthew 5, and apply them to marriage without qualifiers or context, they paint a picture that isn't fully accurate. For example, "Bless those who curse you" sounds a lot like a wife is called to reward her husband when he is demanding or harsh. Or "if someone asks you to go one mile, go with him two." This sounds like if a husband comes home and berates the job his wife did cleaning the bathroom sink, she should rush to clean it again and then scrub the floor on her hands and knees for good measure.

Surely this is not what Jesus had in mind. This kind of loving response to others has a valid place in our Christian life and should guide how we live. But when we take this point and apply it to our marriages in a literal way, we lose balance. Jesus wasn't talking to married couples when he said this, but to the crowds of people who needed to have their entire way of thinking about their enemies and about what love means turned upside down. The principle holds true, but one person consistently applying it in a marriage that lacks mutual love and sacrifice isn't what Jesus intended.

Do not hide naively behind your faith. Rather than struggle to set limits in my marriage, I sometimes hid behind my faith. I stoically claimed Scriptures such as Philippians 4:13, "I can do everything through him who gives me strength," while I gritted my teeth, enduring behavior which should have been lovingly but firmly confronted. I prayed for the Lord's protection when I naively climbed in the car with Randy after he'd been drinking.

Yes, the Lord graciously protected me, and the Scriptures I relied on are an important source of truth and strength. Yet the Lord wants us to act responsibly, not using our faith as a way to bail out, to avoid confrontation and its consequences. The truth is, it's hard to love boldly and to set boundaries, but it's necessary if we're going to honor God's creations: our neighbors and ourselves. Love can and should say no when it's appropriate.

Remember, inviting your husband to treat you or your kids badly is not a sign of virtue or love. It does nothing to help your husband; rather, it reinforces his sin, making your acquiescence anything but a godly response. You could go so far as to say that when a wife accepts a husband's bad behavior toward her in the name of godly submission, she makes a mockery of the sacred picture of Christian marriage that is the union of Christ and the church. When she condones evil against herself or others in the name of Christian love, she is not being spiritual, but naive.

Your actions should be motivated by love. Many wives worry, justifiably, that boundaries taken to extremes will be more hurtful than helpful. Boundaries should always favor good, progress, and people, not just rules for the sake of rules. That means they may need to be set aside in favor of compassion.

"As Jesus has told us, the two greatest commandments hang on the ultimate reality of Love," writes Cloud. "And this is the biggest misunderstanding that we find when talking about boundaries. Many people think that boundaries are about selfishness and are at their root, self-serving. Nothing could be farther from the truth. Boundaries are about freedom, and freedom is always meant to have as its ultimate fruit, love."[2]

It is true that we can get so concerned about our rules, limits, and the protective lines we've drawn that we stop seeing the big picture. We should never forget that boundaries are helpful tools to love one another well, not to be used as weapons or barriers to intimacy.

As you prayerfully consider whether you need to establish some healthy boundaries in your marriage, keep in mind that upbringing and personality play a part in determining how we feel about saying no to someone or setting up limits in our relationships. If your nature and temperament set you up to be a victim, be patient with yourself when it comes to change. Don't feel a need to become someone you aren't or to overhaul your personality overnight.

Likewise, don't get caught in the trap where you are standing on the outside thinking you know exactly what someone else should do. Boundaries are very personal, and when we have tidy formulas for others to follow, we put ourselves in an arrogant position. Just as every person is unique, every marriage is also unique, and the need for boundaries will be different.

It took me a while to gain a balanced understanding of what boundaries are and how they could complement, not compete with, my spiritual goals and God's will for marriage. So if some of the information in this chapter is new to you, sit with it for a while. Ask God to give you wisdom about the issue of boundaries. In the next chapter we'll discuss in more depth how we know when and where to establish boundaries in ways that benefit both your husband and you.

> *Dear Lord,*
> *Thank You that because You gave us free wills, You also gave us the ability to take responsibility for ourselves and our actions. Help me to grow in my understanding of godly and biblical ways of setting boundaries in my marriage. Teach me what is truly helpful and balanced. I want every line I draw in our relationship to reflect my love for my husband and the respect for myself that I know you want each of your children to enjoy. I pray these things in Your name. Amen.*

thirteen

Drawing Lines
with Love

*If you lack wisdom in your relationship with your
husband, ask God to show you what is right. He will
generously give you all the knowledge and insight you
need without finding fault with you or your questions.*

A PARAPHRASE OF JAMES 1:2-5

When I first started to understand the importance of boundaries, I read several books on the topic cover to cover—then
still found myself floundering. I had the basic know-how, but I
needed more insight about the dynamics in my own marriage before
I could implement boundaries that were helpful to me and to Randy.

How do we know when and where to lay down some boundaries in our marriages?

Every wife must wrestle with this question in light of her own
situation and in light of what she believes is going to help her have
a healthy, loving relationship with her spouse. However, there are
some common areas where most relationships benefit from practical and well-established boundaries. Here are some guidelines:

**Set boundaries if you need to protect yourself from feeling like
your husband is taking advantage of you.** Not to say that we can't
offer help, be extravagantly unselfish, or go out of our way to please

our husbands. But if we have healthy boundaries, we will define them according to what we *can* do and *choose* to do. There's a big difference between happily making a sacrifice for someone and feeling taken advantage of by that person.

For example, Janice's husband Martin has friends over every Friday night and leaves a huge mess for Janice to clean the next morning while he's out golfing. If she wants to, Janice can clean up the mess as a favor to her husband or simply because she doesn't mind, and besides, she's happy her husband enjoys his male friends. In this case, Janice's behavior is genuinely loving and sacrificial.

However, if Janice seethes with resentment while she's cleaning up her husband's mess, that's a different story. Her anger and unwillingness indicate that she feels mistreated. She's not *giving* to Martin; she feels something is being exacted from her unfairly. Janice needs to decide on her limits concerning housework and discuss this with her husband. She might explain to him that from now on she will help him clean up, but he must participate and help her. Or she might tell him gently that she feels the situation is unfair, and that from now on, he'll have to clean up the mess when he gets home from golf. Or she might suggest that he take his get-togethers somewhere else.

In one scenario, Janet didn't mind cleaning up after her husband; in the other she resented it. And therein lies the key to knowing when to set boundaries. Our emotions can and do play a role in alerting us to areas where we may need to establish some limits. When you feel one of the following red flag feelings, you likely need to do some boundary setting:

- You feel violated.
- You feel deeply wounded.
- You feel afraid of your husband.

- You feel steeped in resentment.
- You feel powerless.
- You feel anger and rage.

Set boundaries if you need to protect yourself or your children from being mistreaedt, abused, or degraded. Ephesians 5 reminds us that our marriages are a picture of Christ and the church. If that's the case, then your marriage and the rules and limitations that govern it should reflect this. Your boundaries should never be so flimsy as to tolerate harm to you or your kids, for example. Instead, they should promote the ideals of love, respect, and honor. This means that if Nancy's husband insists on calling her children four-letter words when he's angry with them, she should establish a limit or boundary that communicates to her husband that this is *not* acceptable. Maybe she lets her husband know that whenever he blows up this way, she will immediately take the children and leave the house.

Set boundaries if your husband seems to interpret your acts of selflessness or love as signs of weakness or a reason to disrespect you. Your love shouldn't invite your spouse to be inconsiderate, disrespectful, or less mindful of your value as a wife and woman. In other words, when you turn the other cheek, does it prick his conscience, or does it make him feel justified in slapping the other cheek too? Does your recent agreement to let him smoke in the house, for example, cause him to be grateful and considerate, or does it seem to invite even more insensitivity on his part? If so, explain to him that you feel for his sake and yours that you are going to have to adjust some boundaries. Tell him that you really want him to respect you, so you are reevaluating whether your sacrifices to him are healthy on your part and received in a way that's healthy on his part.

It's been said that men dislike a wife that is like a doormat as much as they dislike a dominating one. Be sure to set up boundaries in ways that keep your self-respect and dignity intact.

Set boundaries if your husband is avoiding a problem or addiction. Henry Cloud and John Townsend posed these questions at a workshop: "Who do you know who needs to go through God's school of pain? Are you standing in the way?"

Sometimes if we refuse to set boundaries with our husbands, we keep them from running smack into walls that would help them wake up or force them to deal with a problem. If you are married to a man who has an addiction or some other problem he's in denial about, consider whether your kindness is helping him or hurting him. Ask yourself:

- Does my husband need to hit bottom, and I'm not letting him because of what it will cost me?
- Am I keeping my husband from experiencing the natural consequences of his behaviors?
- Am I protecting my husband from public shame or embarrassment for his sake, or for mine?

Your answers to these questions may help you see more clearly where you stand and what motives are at work. It may be that you need to take your knee pads off your husband's legs, put them back on your own, and then brace for a crash of sorts. Just remember, God will be with you whatever happens. Also, be sure to surround yourself and your husband with resources to help pick up the pieces.

Remember, the reason for boundary setting isn't to get your husband to change his behavior—he may not. Rather, you set boundaries to help you relate to your husband in a way that is emotionally healthy for you and for him.

Again, be sure to be patient with yourself *and with him.*

Sometimes I worried that I'd never get this boundary thing right and that Randy and I would just keep repeating the same patterns into eternity. One woman used to tell me, "You're right where you're

How do I talk to my

husband about

boundaries?

supposed to be right now." I got sick of hearing that, because I wanted to be in a different place—one that didn't hurt so much. It took time, but eventually I began to realize that she was exactly right. I was where I was supposed to be—with Randy, still married, learning how to love him as God does—unconditionally, but also responsibly and wisely.

Boundaries should be clearly communicated to our spouses and, if possible, arrived at by mutual consent and understanding. Here are some guidelines:

As a rule, never propose new boundaries to your husband when you are angry or hurt. For example, screaming in front of a crowd, "That's the very last time I'm ever going to let you make a joke about my weight in public, buster!" It might be justified, but it probably isn't that helpful.

Instead, choose a time when you sense he would be most open to listening and caring and not inclined to take offense.

Explain that you are establishing these boundaries because you love him and want to improve your marriage. Assure him that you aren't trying to push him away or usurp his leadership role. Tell him that you are trying to grow as a person and that you want to take more responsibility for your role in your marriage problems. For example, you might say, "I don't think it's helpful for me to keep being the one responsible for waking you up for work in the mornings. It makes me feel crabby when I have to rouse you numerous times, and it puts me in the position of being responsible for your getting to work on time. For both our sakes, I'm proposing that from now on you set your own alarm and get yourself up. It might help you to know that I'm no longer going to play a part."

Offer to discuss any areas where he might want to establish boundaries of his own with you. As you discuss your growing awareness of the need for boundaries, let your husband know that it's not a one-sided affair. There are probably trouble spots where he needs to set boundaries with you as well. Let him know you're open and that you respect his needs.

Be clear about consequences. Some boundaries require consequences in order to be effective. In other words, if you tell your husband that you will no longer cooperate with his habit of bringing home friends for dinner without giving you any notice, then you need to let him know what will happen if he does this again. Will you politely suggest they dine out? Think through your responses to boundaries you both set and make sure the consequences are clear. Then be sure to follow through.

fourteen

Contentment—It Can Be Habit Forming

A wife in a challenging marriage can be content if
she looks to God for help and strength.

A PARAPHRASE OF PHILIPPIANS 4:13

Practicing contentment. It sounds easy enough. Just like practicing your tennis serve or a musical instrument. When I was
a child, I took piano lessons and had to practice thirty minutes
every day. Most days I resisted, and it was like pulling teeth to get
me to the piano bench. "Practice makes perfect," Mom used to say.
Of course she was right.

If only learning to be content were as rudimentary as practicing scales on the piano, or hitting a can of tennis balls. But contentment, though it can become a habit, isn't a pattern we fall into
easily. Contentment is linked to our hearts and our attitudes, and
they aren't quickly or easily adjusted.

Contentment, especially in our marriages, must be cultivated.
That's no easy task amid media blitz and Hollywood's portrayal of
romantic bliss. Why aren't we going away together for a romantic
weekend to celebrate our anniversary or looking longingly into
each other's eyes over a gourmet dinner? Instead we're eating burg-
ers and fries at a fast-food restaurant, if we even get out at all! It's

> It is always possible to be thankful for what is given rather than to complain about what is not given. One or the other becomes a habit of life.
>
> ELISABETH ELLIOT GREN

tough to continually fight against the current of popular opinion, to not want what we don't have.

So how do we find contentment? Scripture gives us a clue that being content may be difficult, if not impossible, without God's strength. The apostle Paul writes: "For I have learned to be content whatever the circumstances. I know what it is to be in need, and I know what it is to have plenty. I have learned the secret of being content in any and every situation, whether well fed or hungry, whether living in plenty or in want. I can do everything through him who gives me strength" (Philippians 4:11–13).

I've found that one of the greatest antidotes for discontent is gratitude. When I practice seeing what's right, what's good about my marriage, my life, my job, and the day I've just completed, then I can be thankful. Making an ongoing gratitude list can help us in a tangible way to see how God has blessed us. Buy a blank journal, and every night before bed list five things that you're grateful for. They could be basic, permanent fixtures in your life (your children, your home, your health), or they could be something special that happened to you that day, like running into a friend who noticed you lost weight.

In her book *Meditations for Women Who Do Too Much,* Anne Wilson Schaef writes, "Sometimes we feel that if everything isn't perfect, we cannot be grateful for anything. We easily fall into all-or-nothing thinking. When we do, we miss the sunrise and other forms of goodness that surround us. I am grateful. Perhaps that is enough. I am grateful.

"Part of being grateful," she continues, "is developing the ability to accept what cannot be changed and learning to live creatively with those situations."[1]

Julie, mother of two sons and married to her husband, Stan, for twelve years, always felt depressed on special occasions: her birthday, Mother's Day, their anniversary. "I had expectations of what Stan should do for my birthday. Of course, I never clued him in. I thought he'd figure out something special to do—or at least teach our sons to think of me on Mother's Day.

"I used to meet a friend at the local deli on our mutual birthdays. She also struggled with the same problems with her husband. We usually shed a few tears, told each other how much we appreciated our friendship, even if our husbands didn't know exactly how to celebrate special occasions. It wasn't that we expected expensive gifts. We only wanted to be remembered. We wanted to be told, 'You're special.'"

One Mother's Day, Julie decided to make it a special event. She bought a cake and some balloons to decorate the house. Her attitude surprised her. She didn't feel any resentment toward Stan, and she even looked forward to the evening with growing anticipation. When he came in and asked her why the cake and balloons, she simply told him they were going to celebrate Mother's Day. He and their boys gladly joined in. It turned out to be fun. Julie couldn't believe how much her attitude affected everyone—including herself.

She decided then that even if Stan didn't know how to express his feelings, she could be grateful to God for giving her the gift of life on her birthday; and on Mother's Day, she gave thanks for the gift of two beautiful sons.

This isn't a martyr's resignation, but a willingness to embrace our lives, even with the disappointments, and to see the good.

Years later, to celebrate their twentieth anniversary, Stan proudly presented Julie with a new waffle iron. Not exactly the most romantic gift, Julie chuckled, remembering when she practically had to buy her own gifts. But she felt gratitude for all that God had done in her life through the years, teaching her to be content in her marriage.

It was Stan who totally surprised *her*, though. After they finished a romantic anniversary dinner, Stan reached in his pocket and pulled out a tiny, velvet-covered box. Julie gasped. "For me?" Stan nodded with a boyish grin, obviously pleased with himself for pulling it off. He slid toward her a card, which she could hardly read through her tears.

Contentment is freeing. The less you need, the freer you become. The more gratitude you experience for life's precious moments, the more likely you are to find contentment whether you are in need or want. That is a habit worth cultivating.

> *Dear God,*
> *I confess I'm not very grateful for the many blessings*
> *You've given. I take a lot for granted. Help me*
> *practice contentment, even when circumstances in*
> *my marriage are less than ideal. O Lord, giver of all*
> *good gifts, I will start today to give thanks. Before my*
> *feet hit the floor each morning, may I have a prayer*
> *of thanksgiving forming in my heart. Amen.*

VOICES: CORRIE'S STORY

After twenty years of marriage to Sam, Corrie can tell you it still isn't easy being married to a crab, but she rarely has to start her day over anymore. "I feel as if the Lord is continually refining my attitudes, and that makes all the difference."

I remember how difficult it was after Sam and I were first married. He seemed to have a cloud of gloom hanging over him. It depressed me. I would ask him, "What's wrong?" He would say, "Nothing." But his demeanor, the look on his face, the way he walked, how he reacted all made me think he was angry. I allowed his attitude to affect me and make me miserable.

After attending a Christian support group and reading God's Word, I began to see that I was allowing Sam to make me unhappy—but I didn't have to. And if I started feeling miserable, I could start my day over as many times as I needed.

If I wake up in the morning and everything's fine, then things go to "heck in a handbasket," I can say, "Okay, it's 8:00 A.M., I can choose again to be happy." Some days I have to start the day over every forty-five minutes. Other days I start over at 9:00 P.M. This was really difficult at first, and I felt silly. But then I'd say, "This is *my* day. If Sam chooses to

be crabby today, that's *his* choice. I choose to be happy today."

One day we planned a hike in the mountains. I packed a picnic lunch and got the kids' backpacks ready. Sam had gotten up on the wrong side of the bed that morning. I panicked. I dreaded being stuck in the car with him all day. I went to the bedroom, closed the door, and got down on my knees. I read Ephesians 6, about putting on the armor of God. I prayed for the Lord to help me have a good day in spite of Sam's irritable mood.

I had one foot in the car when Sam made another rude remark to me. In that instant I knew what I needed to do. I calmly stated, "Sam, we're not getting along. This isn't going to work for us today. I can't be with you all day in the car when you're treating me this way. Why don't you and the kids go—and have a great time!"

You should have seen Sam's jaw drop. I blew kisses to them all and waved as Sam drove away. I felt peace. I chose to have a good day, to take care of myself by putting up some boundaries.

I knew the kids would be fine with Sam. They came home bubbling with excitement about the fun they had had. Even Sam had a good time and his mood improved.

Starting your day over is simply a matter of changing your attitude and getting your eyes back on the Lord. This practice has become so ingrained in me that even when Sam is irritable, deep in my heart I feel inner joy and peace in spite of his behavior. I know the only way I can do this is by getting close to the Lord, reading and applying His word. It took some time, but most days I'm able to say, "I'm really feeling joy. I'm having a good day today."

fifteen

Marriage Is Blind

Like an apple tree among the trees of the forest is my husband among all men. I delight to spend time with him, and his kisses are sweet to my taste. Strengthen me with raisins, refresh me with apples, for I am faint with love.

A PARAPHRASE OF SONG OF SONGS 2:3, 5

owsa. When was the last time you were "faint with love"? Do you remember what it felt like?

When we first fell in love with our husbands, it was thumping hearts and romance and bliss. We were convinced we'd found the utterly perfect match. We didn't see their faults, imperfections, addictions, or bad habits. We even imagined that their weaknesses, if they had any, would be insignificant, endearing, even becoming....

Almost all of us begin here. An amazing blindness to the ordinary is the magic dust of a budding romance. Then marriage opens our eyes. In time, we come to see our mates more realistically.

Or do we? What if romantic love isn't blind at all? What if that first dazzling image we have of the other is the real truth, the truest glimpse of our mate we'll ever have? Maybe it's not love that makes us blind and marriage that makes us see. Maybe it's actually in marriage that we become truly blind. Blind to the wonder, glory, and mystery of our mate. Blind to the incredible person that God made and God sees.

Think about it. Doesn't God see glory in His children? Isn't this the way God sees our mates and us—through the blood of His Son, minus our sins and shortcomings?

In fact, it was being seen this way that made our romance so wonderful. When you first fell in love with your husband, you were drawn to him partly because of how he saw you. You liked your reflection in his eyes. He seemed to see and appreciate all that you were and would become and to even pull you toward your best self.

Nowadays, chances are that you don't like how he sees you. And most likely he feels the same about how you see him. You no longer look at him like he's your hero. You see his failures and faults and broken promises. Neither of you is seeing the other as God does.

But here's the good news. You've probably been blinded by making these three marriage mistakes, all of which are correctable:

You become blind to each other's potential to become more than you are. In romance, you imagine that the glorious creature you adore is bound only for more glorious growth—greater faith, increased expressions of talents, enhanced ability to love. You share his dreams for all he will become. But then after a few years—or months!—he's no longer growing and changing before your eyes, fascinating you with his potential.

And what happens then? Very often he senses your conclusion and agrees. He settles in. He abandons his dreams. He'll never be anything more than he already is. Now, it's just a matter of getting older. When he looks in your eyes, he sees proof positive: *She's right. I'm a finished product.*

How can you reverse this loss of vision? Probably the most important thing you can do is look for ways to send these kinds of messages to your husband:

"God isn't done with you yet."

"You are getting better and better at _____."

"It's going to be interesting to see where you're at and how you've changed in five years."

"I believe in you and all you are still becoming."

As you affirm your husband's great potential for growth and change, chances are that he will begin to catch some of the vision. He'll feel the need to see himself through your eyes. And when he sees a man full of untapped potential and talent, the possibilities become limitless.

You become blind to each other's mysteries. One of the most delightful aspects of courtship is the promise of discovery. You looked into your future husband's eyes and saw things you couldn't wait to explore more. You wanted to know everything about him: his childhood, his favorite things, his philosophies on life.

But because of the intimate knowledge that comes from living with someone day in and day out, you begin to see your spouse in a one-dimensional way. You think you've covered every acre of his personality. You unconsciously conclude that you know all there is to know—the mystery is gone.

But your husband is more than he appears or you can presently see. He is more than he's told you. And when you look at him as if what you see is all there is of him, it crushes his spirit. Of course, the same is true if and when your husband decides he knows all there is to know and stops exploring who you are.

Maybe it's time for you to pursue knowing your husband once again. Explore the terrain of his soul with a sincere desire to discover something more, something wonderful. Look at him with expectation and awe. Look at him through new eyes, eyes that assume there's more here than meets the eye.

In *The Mystery of Marriage,* Mike Mason advises: "You must

start over again in your mysteries. He is a mystery to you. And you want to be a mystery to him. There is a lot more to you than meets his eyes, he must know that. So you can share each other's private demons and secret angels and leave yourselves room for wonder at one another."[1]

You become blind to each other's heroic qualities. You might read those words and think, *I used to think he had some of those....* Maybe you can remember making lists of your husband-to-be's wonderful qualities and mooning over them. Now you list the pros and cons of staying.

But think about it for a minute. If you don't see your husband's heroic qualities, it's because you're not looking for them. They're still there. Make a list of all the things that make life hard for your husband. It might be his job, a lack of education, a father who was absent, a personality that's challenging. Then list his broken dreams. What has not happened in his life that he dreamed of? Then list the small and big disappointments he's encountered. Then list what you think he feels about himself as a husband. Are you beginning to see a hero emerge?

Karen, a mother of three, tells this story: "One morning my husband let his alarm go off again and again. He knows I hate that. He has to be at work by 6 A.M. and I don't want to wake up that early. He finally turns it off and gets up, but I can't get back to sleep. A few minutes later, he comes out of the shower and starts fishing around in his drawer, looking for socks. He can't find any. I peek at him, not letting him know I'm awake. It's my fault there are no socks. Finally he digs out a pair from the dirty laundry and sits on the side of the bed and begins putting them on.

"I stare at his back, and for some reason, I begin to have empathetic thoughts: *This back carries a large load. This back worries about our credit card debt. This back bends over to hug kids that he's pretty sure he's failing somehow. This back comes home every night to a wife who's not sure she really loves him, at least not like she used to.* Suddenly my heart broke for him. I thought about his life, all his disadvantages, the story he tells of his father driving away after the divorce and never coming back. As he slipped on his clothing in the dark and then tried to shut the bedroom door behind him as quietly as possible, I suddenly realized I was married to a hero. A flawed, frustrating, maddening hero. But a hero nonetheless."

Do any of these blind mistakes ring a bell? God is inviting you out of your blindness. He wants to give you His eyes to see your husband as He does: still growing and changing, brimming with mystery, and possessing great heroic potential, no matter how squashed it's become.

You are your husband's mirror. You are the one who says how you view him: "This is what you look like." You have the power, with God's help, to give your husband a new perspective on his present worth and future hope.

> *Dear Lord,*
> *Help me see my husband's heroic qualities. He may*
> *fail miserably. He may fight demons daily that he*
> *can't seem to beat. But he is first of all doing his best*
> *with what he has to work with. Help me to*
> *remember his disadvantages, his wounds, his broken*
> *parts. Help me to see past the mistakes he makes, the*
> *way he hurts me, the many times he doesn't live up*
> *to what I want. Give me eyes to see my husband*
> *exactly the way You see him, Lord—as a hero in*
> *disguise. Amen.*

sixteen

When the Grass
Looks Greener

*When you thirst for love, don't go looking for it
outside your marriage. Why should you indulge in
acts or fantasies that will only make you miserable?
Instead, let your heart, thoughts, and body belong to
your husband alone. Then your intimacy with him
will be blessed by God, and you'll find joy in the
husband He gave you. Why be captivated, my
daughter, by the appeal of adultery? Why embrace,
in deed or even in thought, the arms of another man?*

A PARAPHRASE OF PROVERBS 5:15–18, 20

Marcia had been attending a women's Bible study at her church for almost a year. But she'd hesitated to talk about how painful her marriage was. Then one afternoon, while the group was studying Proverbs, the passage at the top of this page came up. Marcia decided it was time to be honest. "I hate to say it," she announced, "but I think my well has gone sour. My fountain doesn't feel blessed—my husband isn't even interested in it. I have no reason to rejoice in my husband. And actually, it's really easy to be captivated by other men. If I ever slept with one, I could write a long list of very good reasons why I did it."

96

The group was silent. No one quite knew what to say to Marcia's honest outburst. Finally the leader said, "I'm so sorry, Marcia, that it feels that way for you. I can't say that I fully understand. Probably none of us here can know exactly what you go through in your marriage. But we all care. And we will all pray for you and Rob."

Later, during the final prayer time, Marcia began to weep. When it came her turn to pray, she let out a torrent of grief and anger over her circumstances. She raged at God for several minutes about all that was wrong with her marriage and how much she wanted a new husband who would be more loving. After her sobs subsided, the rest of the group laid their hands on her and prayed for her. Before she left, she said, "I've never felt more cleansed and hopeful. I really needed to get that out. I needed to say it to God and then know He still loved me and that He still cared."

Maybe you can identify with Marcia's feelings. Sometimes the idea of seeking solace in the arms of another man can be tempting, especially if a particular man comes to mind. A discontented wife can suddenly become much more than discontented when an attractive man comes along and shows even the slightest interest in her. Suddenly what was a hard marriage begins to feel impossible, and a difficult period in a relationship escalates into a dangerous flirtation with the idea of divorce and remarriage.

If you are in a difficult marriage, sooner or later you'll be tempted to think about how much happier you might be with another man. How do you handle these very real feelings? You know they're wrong. You know what the Bible says about adultery. But you ache inside to experience the kind of affection that resides just over the fence. What can you do? *Have a preventive plan.* Here are some tips to put to work:

Admit to yourself that it's possible there is a man out there that you could be happier with. (I warned you that this book would be different from other Christian books you've read on marriage!) Like me, you've probably heard a lot of sermons on the myth of the greener grass. In terms of marriage, the phrase refers to a spouse's faulty belief that he would be happier and that life would be better with someone else. This is called a myth because life will not be better with another person. Supposedly there isn't really another man who would meet your needs in the ways you imagine. Even if he looked the perfect part, once you got to know him, you'd discover rambling weeds and brown patches, difficulties and problems a lot like the ones you experience now.

However, this isn't always as much of a myth as we'd like to think. Let's face it. Sometimes the grass really is greener on the other side, at least in some important spots. You might meet a man who is single, who is a Christian, who would love you and cherish you and treat you better than your current husband. There would be less fighting, fewer disappointments. Yes, there'd be dry spells and trouble now and then, but all in all, the grass would be greener. Maybe you even think you've seen it happen for others.

Obviously you won't successfully combat the temptation to have an affair or leave your husband if you convince yourself a better guy is not out there. That plan will fall apart when Mr. Wonderful comes along and you just can't believe that the grass over there isn't greener. The best plan to avoid this temptation is the one that will work even if a man should come along who, by all accounts and purposes, has the greenest grass you've ever seen.

Remember you have an enemy. Perhaps the greatest key to remember is that you have an actual enemy who hates your marriage. This excerpt from Randy Alcorn's book, *Lord Foulgrin's Letters*, illustrates how Satan schemes to take down marriages. In the following excerpt, one demon is talking to another about how to trip up a wife:

Tired of a man who'd rather push buttons on a remote control than listen to her, she's on the prowl for Prince Charming. Patty seeks a man of nobility who wants nothing more than to gaze into her eyes, write her love notes, take her to the most expensive and exciting places, and make her feel wonderful. Never mind no such man exists. Never mind if he did exist he'd have better things to do than fawn over her.... Fletcher is her most recent perfect man. He's her imaginary lover, an idol fashioned by her hands. He stands in perpetual contrast to her bumbling, belching husband. Never mind her husband works hard, loves the children, and is kind to her, kinder than most men she could hope to marry, including Fletcher....

Soon Patty will jump over [God's] guardrails in her quest for freedom. She'll experience it too, for about ten seconds, as she falls off the cliff. Later, after she's burned her bridges behind her, the divorce is final, and her children no longer trust her...she'll cry out, "Why did You let this happen to me, God?" Those are glorious scenes, are they not? They choose to jump over [God's] guardrails, then blame Him for it. Splendid.[1]

Know where you are vulnerable. There is no woman more susceptible to an affair—of the heart or flesh—than a woman in an unfulfilling marriage. The wonder of being wanted, the power of feeling your power over another, the thrill of knowing someone desires you, wants to explore your thoughts, and thinks you're amazing is heady stuff. Rather than denying you are at all vulnerable, be honest about those areas where you might be weak and ask God to strengthen you.

Sally, for example, doesn't think she's capable of an affair. When she flirts with Harry at work, she tells herself that she's just trying to feel validated. She just wants to prove to herself that she could still attract a man. But because she thinks she's stronger than she is, Sally has put herself at high risk of an affair. Beware of doing the same.

Watch out for the "better guy." A lot of women imagine that if they ever had an affair, it would be with some man they don't know, a hero who comes out of nowhere. But in reality, Prince Charming is much more likely to be someone familiar, someone they already know. Be wary of these common traps:

- The good friend who's a guy but "understands you almost as well as your girlfriends."
- A male mentor. Shared interests are a powerful pull. And so is the allure of a man who knows more than you about something you love.
- A close friend's husband. Sounds awful, doesn't it? But it happens again and again. The opportunities for too much intimacy abound when couples spend lots of time together.
- A coworker. Again, who understands your stress and your challenges better than someone at work? Not to mention the convenient and often close proximity that some careers afford, especially if they include travel.
- A pastor or counselor. Sad but true, many pastors have fallen into adultery. It happens at church. It happens to the best. We are all in need, all broken. And some of the most caring, wonderful men in the world are Christians. But they are still men.

Count the cost. Sometimes an affair breaks up a marriage and the two lovers get together. But the guilt and trauma forever associated with their affair tends to make a long-term relationship all but impossible. Deanna's adulterous affair with Jim came to light after Jim told Deanna that their relationship would last forever. They agreed to tell their spouses. Deanna ended her marriage with her husband, Nathan. And Jim broke the news to his wife as well. But in the ensuing months, as reality slammed into their families, as their kids cried, as relatives pleaded…the pretty plan fell apart. Jim repented and reconciled with his wife, and the couple moved out of town to start over. Nathan divorced Deanna. Today she's a single mom and bitter. "I feel like the woman they talk about in Proverbs who tore down her house with her own hands…all I wanted was love. All I got was loneliness."

Establish some boundaries. Every wife will have personal feelings about what is appropriate for her, but here are some safety measures wise women have put in place:

- Don't hug other men besides your husband or male relatives.
- Don't have meals alone with another man.
- Don't read books or watch movies that glorify affairs or downplay the consequences.
- Dress in such a way as not to send sexual signals to men.
- Don't establish an intimate friendship with another man that doesn't include your husband.
- Don't participate in "harmless" sexual jokes or innuendos.
- Tell your husband immediately if a man appears obviously interested in you or you in him.

As you pray about this issue or offer help to a struggling friend, remember that what matters isn't determining whether or not the grass is really greener. It's about saying, "I want my grass, no matter how brown and blasted by storms it might get, to be blessed by God. I chose this man, and I won't be tricked into betraying him." Stand your ground, and God will stand with you. And you will never be sorry.

Dear Lord,
I want to be faithful in every way—in body,
emotions, mind, spirit, and imagination—to the
husband You have given me. You have said,
"Marriage should be honored by all, and the
marriage bed kept pure" (Hebrews 13:4). Show me
anything in my life today that threatens the
refreshing purity You want for me. Help me to be
true in all I do. Amen.

seventeen

I Surrender All

Don't put your trust in your own understanding,
opinions, or attempts to control your husband. Instead,
with all your heart surrender everything to God,
trusting Him to lead both of you down the right path.

A PARAPHRASE OF PROVERBS 3:5

Randy and I had gone rafting with friends, and we were enjoying majestic mountain scenes and warm spring sunshine. In an instant, our float trip turned into a nightmare. A swift runoff current caught our raft and propelled it toward a logjam. Randy screamed at me to paddle harder, but we couldn't avoid the collision. Our raft exploded as we hit the tree. We plunged into glacial water; the current crushed both of us against a limb.

Randy struggled to free himself. The panic in his voice terrified me. Finally he managed to push away from the log. I watched him being swept downstream. He grabbed a branch and hung on, then slowly clawed his way onto the tree trunk. I dug my fingernails into the limb, afraid to let go.

"Deb, you have to let go so I can get you out."

"No, no—I can't do it. I'm too scared." My teeth chattered.

"Let go of the limb, Deb," Randy instructed, his voice now steady and calm. "You'll only be underwater a few seconds. I'll catch you when you come out on the other side."

I knew I didn't have any choice. My only hope was to let go; otherwise I would remain trapped by the relentless current and be overcome by hypothermia. With such cold water, that could take only a matter of minutes. Finally I released my grip. Raging water tumbled over me. With what seemed to me like Herculean strength, Randy grabbed my arms and yanked me to safety.

As I healed from the bumps and bruises of our river adventure, I thought of how difficult it was for me to let go of Randy and the expectations I had of him and our marriage. Just as I had hung on in the river, too terrified to let go, I had clung to my illusion of control in our marriage, afraid that if I stopped hanging on to what I wanted, our marriage would die.

When I first realized that Randy had a drinking problem, I launched a personal crusade to get him sober, to "fix" him. I pleaded, plotted, nagged, bargained, and scolded. I believed that if he became a Christian, our lives would surely improve. I left books in strategic places, covered the refrigerator with message magnets, and coerced him into attending church services.

In fact, a friend and I had the audacity to plan the evening when we knew our husbands would become believers! A well-known evangelist was speaking at a local church. If only Randy could hear him and the gospel message—how could he not respond? To our dismay, the evening turned out to be a complete disaster. My friend's husband left the service during the altar call. Randy stuck it out but lambasted me afterward. He told me in no uncertain terms that he wasn't interested in becoming a Christian. He had reluctantly obliged me by going to church before, but only to get me off his case. Not surprisingly, he didn't become a Christian for many years—nor did he stop drinking.

The day Randy finally checked into an alcohol treatment center, I rejoiced with exhausted relief. But I soon realized that his sobriety was tenuous.

Once again I tried to ensure that Randy didn't resume drinking. I was walking on eggshells, avoiding conflicts, trying my best to provide a stress-free environment because I feared it might cause Randy to start drinking again. I fell into bed at night, weary and anxious. But despite all my efforts, Randy did start drinking again. I spiraled into despair and resentment, more determined than ever to be in control.

Step out in faith. Be willing to take the chance—God won't fail us. We might have a small faith, but we have a big God!

NED GRAHAM

Oh, how human it is to want to be in control of our lives and the lives of those close to us. Yielding our wills, accepting that control is an illusion, and trusting God with our husbands is difficult.

Anne Wilson Schaef writes in *Meditations for Women Who Do Too Much:* "Our illusion of control dies very slowly. The more changing and uncertain our lives are, the more we fall back on our favorite illusion that if we can just get in charge, we can control everything. Letting go of our illusion of control in even the smallest way reverberates throughout our lives."[1]

How, then, do we let go?

Admit that you struggle with accepting what is. It helped me to admit to myself and God that much of my struggle with control comes from wanting my own agenda. I struggle with accepting that my marriage is not what I had hoped and prayed it would be. Acceptance is key to finding peace and contentment despite our circumstances.

Ask God to help you change the things you can and to accept the things you can't. Surrendering means focusing on changing yourself and giving up changing your husband. We can make David's prayer our own: "Search me, O God, and know my heart; test me and know my anxious thoughts. See if there is any offensive way in me, and lead me in the way everlasting" (Psalm 139:23–24).

If you are like me, some of your own behaviors are contributing to your dissatisfaction in your marriage. As I asked God to search my heart, He began to show me that I had a lot of unrealistic expectations about Randy and our marriage—I expected my husband to meet all my needs. God also gave me the grace to let go of those expectations...it didn't happen overnight, but it happened. When we let go of these expectations, we stop trying to control our husbands.

A friend once told me, "Faith is walking to the edge of what we know—then taking one more step." Oswald Chambers writes: "Do you believe in a miracle-working God, and will you go out in surrender to Him until you are not surprised an atom at anything He does? Suppose God is the God you know Him to be when you are nearest Him...what an impertinence worry is!"[2]

Surrender is an act of faith. It means trusting that the One who made your mate is the One who can change him.

Dear God,
I admit I am obsessed with controlling my husband.
I'm too afraid not to. What if our marriage ends in
divorce? What if my worst nightmares happen? What
then? I admit I can't control anyone else. I believe
You are in control. As an act of my will, I surrender
my will to Yours. Please give me courage to risk, to
become vulnerable. I will entrust my husband and
our marriage to You, not my limited resources. I
won't allow my fears to interfere with what You want
for my life. I am not in control. What a relief! Amen.

eighteen

I Married a Fool

*When your husband is acting like a fool, don't
respond by stooping to his level, or you will become
like him.*

A PARAPHRASE OF PROVERBS 26:4

ou might call Abigail the patron saint of wives in difficult
marriages. The Bible says of Abigail, "She was an intelligent
and beautiful woman, but her husband [Nabal], a Calebite, was
surly and mean in his dealings" (1 Samuel 25:3). One of their ser-
vants says of Nabal, "He is such a wicked man that no one can talk
to him" (1 Samuel 25:17). In yet another scene, Nabal is described
as "in high spirits and very drunk" (1 Samuel 25:36).

You can read Abigail's story in 1 Samuel 25. To summarize:
David has been on the run from Saul. He and his small army of
men have been camped near Nabal's sheep and herders. Unaware
of the kind of man Nabal is, David sends a message to Nabal, point-
ing out that it is sheep-shearing time. And, since his men have
treated Nabal's herders well, David asks if Nabal would be inclined
to share some of his goods with David and his men.

Nabal refuses and insults David. "Who is this guy? A nobody!
Why should I share with him?"

When David hears this, he's so enraged that he sets out with his men to slaughter Nabal and every male in his household.

This is where Abigail comes into the picture. When she discovers what her foolish husband has done, she realizes that she must act quickly and wisely. She is, after all, caught between two angry men who are acting rashly. (David, though no one's fool, was definitely acting like one in the heat of vengeance.)

Abigail immediately puts together some provisions for David and his men, mounts a donkey, and rides out to meet them. She then delivers a moving speech to David and dissuades him from his plan of vengeance. Abigail returns home to a drunk Nabal and waits until morning to tell him what she's done. When he hears the news, "His heart failed him and he became like a stone" (1 Samuel 25:37). About ten days later, he dies. Soon after, David returns for Abigail to make her his wife.

Does this story sound familiar? Maybe even now you find yourself in Abigail's position: Your husband has rashly done something that is bound to hurt your entire family. You don't know what to do, how to intervene, or even if you should act on it. Women who are married to difficult men can learn a lot from Abigail's interactions with both Nabal and David.

Abigail's response to her husband's rashness demonstrates an important principle: *When physical danger looms, act wisely.* Abigail lost no time protecting her sons and the rest of the male household. She moved quickly. She could have caved in to fear and believed that she had no options. She could have said to Nabal, "You stupid idiot! Now we're all going to die!" Instead, she bravely put herself at risk (David and his men could have taken out their rage at Nabal on her) and trusted God to help her intervention succeed.

When Kelli's husband stopped paying all the bills so he'd have money for gambling in nearby Las Vegas, she decided to take action. After all, she and her three small children needed money for food and medical visits and other necessities. Because Patrick always cashed his paycheck and hid the money, Kelli felt her only option was to ask Patrick's boss to let her pick up the check instead of giving it to her husband so she could have a portion. The boss agreed to the new arrangement and stood up to Patrick when he angrily demanded his check. Now Kelli deposits some of the check each month in a separate account to cover living expenses and hands over to Patrick what's left. Her actions were risky, but under the circumstances she acted as wisely as she could in a difficult situation.

A second principle we can glean from Abigail is this: *In your acting, remain loyal to your husband.* You can't help but wonder how such a beautiful and intelligent woman could stand to be married to a wicked, foolish man who was also stupid—so stupid that he almost got his household murdered by David's army. Didn't Abigail want to escape the marriage? She could have begged David, "Spare my sons! But please, please…go ahead and get rid of my husband!"

But she didn't. Instead, she went to David and said, "Let the blame be on me alone!" When her wicked husband finally died, it was neither by her hand nor David's. God rescued her from her marriage and gave her a second chance, a chance she wouldn't have gotten had she seized upon it herself.

How can a wife like Kelli honor a husband like Patrick when she's going through his boss to divert his paycheck? Kelli says, "In order to protect Patrick's reputation, I was careful not to tell Patrick's boss details about his gambling problem or why I needed to take such a drastic measure. When Patrick was yelling at me after discovering what I'd done, I tried to stay calm. I told him I didn't want to disrespect him, and I assured him that plenty of households operated this way—the wife gets an allowance, but the husband controls the rest. 'After all,' I said, 'It's your money and I know you work hard for it.' This seemed to appease him somewhat—calling my part an allowance and acknowledging he worked for it let him keep some kind of dignity he needed."

If you, like Abigail and Kelli, find yourself or your kids threatened by your husband's foolish choices, try to remember these tips for action:

- Don't wait and hope for the best; take decisive action.
- If you need professional help to accomplish an intervention of some kind, seek it.
- Tell your husband calmly what you've done when the time is right (Abigail was wise not to talk to Nabal while he was drunk).
- Pray for wisdom and talk through your plans with someone else.

Now, before we look at what we can learn from Abigail's interaction with David, we need to ask: What did Nabal do to make David so furious?

Remember, David has been on the run from King Saul. Even though he's been anointed the next king, instead of ascending to the throne, he's been forced to live like an outlaw. He's tired, discouraged, wondering if the prophet Samuel made a big mistake when he thought David was God's choice for king. Then Nabal comes along and says, "Who is this David? Who is this son of Jesse? He's nothing more than a common marauder. Why would I share my food with him?"

It is a direct hit to David's tender ego. His pride deeply stung, he sets out to take vengeance.

So what does Abigail say to David when she finally meets up with rash, angry man number two?

When Abigail saw David, she quickly got off her donkey and bowed down before David with her face to the ground. She fell at his feet and said, "My lord, let the blame be on me alone. Please let your servant speak to you; hear what your servant has to say.

Now since the LORD has kept you, my master, from bloodshed and from avenging yourself with your own hands, as surely as the LORD lives and as you live, may your enemies and all who intend to harm my master be like Nabal. And let this gift, which your servant has brought to my master, be given to the men who follow you. Please forgive your servant's offense, for the LORD will certainly make a lasting dynasty for my master, because he fights the LORD's battles. Let no wrongdoing be found in you as long as you live. Even though someone is pursuing you to take your life, the life of my master will be bound securely in the bundle of the living by the LORD your God. But the lives of your enemies he will hurl away as from the pocket of a sling. When the LORD has done for my master every good thing he promised concerning him and has appointed him leader over Israel, my master will not have on his conscience the staggering burden of needless bloodshed or of having avenged himself. And when the LORD has brought my master success, remember your servant. (1 Samuel 25:23–24; 26–31)

Notice the elements of Abigail's moving speech. She humbles herself, affirms David's feelings of outrage, and reaffirms his integrity. She reminds him that no one, not even a dumb man like Nabal, can come between David and God's great plans for him. Then she gently points out to him that if he sheds innocent blood, because he is

God's chosen and a righteous man, he will regret it later.

Her words quelled David's wrath, and they won his respect as well as his heart. There is nothing more powerful than when a woman says to a man: "I see who you are. I believe in you and in your dream. I think you are going to do the right thing. God is with you and you will succeed."

> Some women make a fool out of a man, but many a godly woman has made a man out of a fool.
>
> ANONYMOUS

David responds to Abigail by saying, "Praise be to the LORD, the God of Israel, who has sent you today to meet me. May you be blessed for your good judgment and for keeping me from bloodshed this day and from avenging myself with my own hands" (1 Samuel 25:32–33).

Can you remember a time when your husband, like David, has felt under siege? In an emotional desert? On the verge of doing something foolish? At such times you can be like Abigail: a wise and loving intervener. Rather than begging or arguing to make him see your side, help him see his own side more clearly. When your husband is making a rash decision, try Abigail's approach:

Affirm his past victories. Did you notice Abigail's reference to a sling? She is letting David know that she is aware of his past heroics and that his past is a sure reflection of his future. Today you might say to your husband something like, "I still remember that time when you…" or "I know you've faced challenges like this before and that now you'll succeed again."

Affirm his integrity. Abigail reminded David that he was only the warrior; the battle belonged to the Lord. So don't compromise. "Let no wrongdoing be found in you," she urged (v. 28). This could be said to your husband as simply, "I know you want to do the right thing…"

Affirm his calling and destiny. Abigail reminded David of his life purpose—"the LORD will certainly make a lasting dynasty for my master" (v. 28). Say to your husband, "I know God has great plans to use you," or, if he's not a Christian, "I know that you have special gifts and that you can do something important with your life…"

Affirm God's faithfulness. Abigail reminded David that God can be trusted even when circumstances look terrible—"The life of my master will be bound securely in the bundle of the living by the LORD your God" (v. 29). Your husband might respond to words such as, "I know that if you trust God He'll never let you down…."

Affirm his future success. Abigail tells him that she believes in him, that he will get there if he holds on. "When the LORD has brought my master success, remember your servant" (v. 31).

By then it's likely that David was thinking, *Forget a woman like you?*

When your husband is in danger of losing his way, the truth about who he is and what he's meant to be is one of love's most beautiful and unforgettable gifts. In fact, it's a gift you shouldn't reserve for emergencies.

> *Dear Lord,*
> *When my husband is acting like a fool, help me not*
> *to be one, too. It's so easy to lose my own head when*
> *he loses his. Help me to be like Abigail—ready to*
> *risk myself in order to save him from his own foolish*
> *choices. May I be discreet, as wise, as noble as she*
> *was. I need Your help to do that, Lord. Please tap me*
> *on the shoulder in the moment of crisis. Please*
> *whisper in my ear what to say, what to do. And I will*
> *do my best to obey. Amen.*

VOICES: JACKIE'S STORY

Jackie and her husband Larry have been married for three years. Long enough, Jackie says, to figure out what a jerk Larry is. She struggles with the idea of respecting a husband who isn't very respectable. But when she finally faced her dilemma head on, she discovered that God sees Larry differently than she does.

It may not sound nice, but Larry is what you'd call a complete jerk. I mean, the entire package: verbally abusive, a problem drinker, arrogant beyond belief, and an absentee dad to the children he had with the wife previous to me. Around the house, this man wouldn't so much as make himself a sandwich if he were starving. Clean up? He told me to get a part-time job so I could hire someone to do whatever it was I wanted him to do.

When we got married, I didn't know the Lord, and I didn't really know my husband either. After coming to Christ a couple of years ago, I kept hearing all this stuff about honoring Larry, submitting to Larry.... And I'd think, *Are you serious?*

A few weeks ago our women's Bible study was studying in Ephesians. When we got to the verse, "Let the wife see that she respects her husband," I knew everyone was thinking of Larry. They all know I'm in an unhappy marriage, so I finally just blurted out: "How do you respect a husband you don't really respect? Someone help me understand how you honor a guy like my husband."

Jackie's Story

An uncomfortable silence ensued. "Well," Karla, the group leader finally said, "let's talk about that. Does anyone have any insight to share?"

Finally a woman named Marsha spoke up. "I think you have to think about how the word *respect* doesn't mean the same thing as *approve* or *condone*. You have to separate what Larry does from who Larry is. You can respect his position, just like you respect a cop who pulls you over, even though you don't like what he's doing to you."

That made sense to me. Sort of. But could I somehow find a way to respect and honor Larry simply because he's my husband?

That afternoon as I was chopping carrots to add to a roast, I continued to debate with myself. Let's say I did decide to honor Larry because God says to and because God loves him. By honoring him, wouldn't I be telling him, "You're perfectly okay how you are—I think you're just wonderful because God loves you"?

Later, after dinner had been cleaned up and Larry had become one with his recliner, I went to our bedroom to read a novel. The main character was a man who was everything I could want in a husband and the exact opposite of Larry. The contrast was painful. Finally, I put the book down and began to pray halfheartedly for Larry. I tried to picture him as God sees him. But that wasn't working. Larry, after all, isn't wearing Christ's robes.

I kept at it, though, and then something happened. Suddenly all this grief welled up, and I sensed it was not mine, but God's. It was like He was crying—over Larry! I'm not the type of person to see things or hear God when I pray. So I asked God what this meant and waited. It began to dawn on me that when God sees Larry, He sees a son of His who won't come home. He sees the marvelous man Larry could be, would be, if he would only let love break through.

Larry doesn't behave in ways that deserve my respect. But the Larry God loves, who's buried behind that brick wall, does. Now I am trying really hard, every day, to feel God's grief over, and love for, Larry. I keep looking for ways to show him respect. I ask his opinions about things that I never used to before. I listen carefully to what he says and I make eye contact when he's talking to me. I tell him I'm proud of him when anything good happens at work. And I don't grumble and complain about him to my friends every day.

As I'm doing this, I'm realizing something important. Respect is a man's number one love language. You should have seen the look on his face a few days ago when I asked Larry what I could do to show him more respect. He was so stunned, he was speechless for once.

Then yesterday I caught myself thinking, *Larry seems to appreciate having my respect, but I still don't know if this is going to work.* I had to quickly remind myself that it's not supposed to work. Changing Larry isn't the goal. That would only turn what I'm doing into manipulation.

I can honor Larry because God asks me to. Buried deep inside of him is a man worthy of respect. And for now, that's good enough for me. The rest is up to Larry and God.

nineteen

Marriage as Ministry

*Whatever you do for your husband, whether it is
something kind you say, a chore you do, or a sacrifice
you make, go about it as if you are doing it not just
for him, but for Jesus; then you will be able to do it
with a thankful heart.*

A PARAPHRASE OF COLOSSIANS 3:17

In his book *The Marriage Builder,* Larry Crabb points out
that as long as we see marriage as an arrangement to meet our
deepest relational needs, we'll be tempted to manipulate our mate
to meet those needs. He suggests that instead we view our marriage
as a ministry.

Amazing, isn't it, that when you say the word *ministry,* the last
person you tend to think of is your husband? Maybe you have a
ministry to the homeless. Or maybe you have a healing ministry
among the women in your church. But your husband?

Crabb writes, "Husbands and wives are to regard marriage as
an opportunity to minister in a unique and special way to another
human being, to be used of God to bring their spouses into a more
satisfying appreciation of their worth as persons who are secure and
significant in Jesus Christ."[1]

We are all familiar with the idea that we are Christ's body on earth—His hands, His feet. It is through us that He reaches out to the world. But it's easy to forget that we are Christ's hands and feet to our husbands.

That's why seeing your marriage as ministry may require an intentional shift of perspective from that of just a wife to that of a woman with a specific ministry to a specific man.

Actually, in God's eyes, ministering to our husbands is *not* optional. Our families are the only mission field we can be absolutely sure God has called us to. It's earth shattering when you think about it: I am God's appointed lover of my husband's soul. I am the only one on earth, the one and only person God made to love my husband in a way that mirrors Christ's love. I was not given to my husband so that I could change him or manipulate him into meeting my needs. But to minister to him.

Crabb writes,

> From a human perspective, three elements are required to shift from manipulation to ministry:
> • A decisive and continuous willingness to adopt the commitment to minister;
> • A substantial awareness of your partner's needs;
> • A conviction that you are God's chosen instrument to touch those needs. [2]

Notice his words: *decisive, continuous, willingness, commitment.* In order to turn your marriage into a real ministry to your husband, you have to be intentional. Marriage as ministry doesn't happen automatically any more than ministry to others outside your home does. Here are some suggestions to help you make that leap:

Change the way you think about physical tasks in your marriage. A key part of ministering to someone is meeting not just his spiritual needs, but also his physical needs. But this can be harder to do with your husband than with a stranger. If you bring meals to shut-ins as part of your ministry, you don't expect anything in return. And there's no emotional cost to you—these people appear wholly deserving and none of them have made your life difficult. You enjoy setting out to meet someone's need on behalf of Jesus.

But how easy it is to come home that same night and whine while you cook dinner and resent that you are also left to clean it up. That doesn't *feel* like ministry. That feels like being a maid.

But what if you were to do things for your husband as an act of ministry? As unto the Lord Himself?

It sounds so silly, so simple, doesn't it? "Do it for Jesus." However, if you were to take the words to heart and act them out, I think you'd be amazed. Not necessarily by your husband's response, but by your own change of heart. Think about how it would change your perspective if every sock you folded was for Jesus. If every dish you loaded was for Jesus. If every extra mile you went, you did it for Jesus. If every time you turned your cheek, it was for Jesus. If every time you sacrificed yourself in any way, you sacrificed for Jesus.

Employ the basic tools of ministry. Much of what we do when we minister is motivated by an awareness of those needs we all have. You can always minister to your husband by:

- Praying and/or fasting for him, especially for growth in his spiritual life.
- Loving him selflessly and being generous with your affections. Yes, hugs can be ministry and so can lovemaking (in fact, ministering to him through sex might be at the top of his list!).

- Being an encourager. For example, you might say, "Benny, I've noticed that you are really working hard on controlling your temper."
- Affirming his gifts. You can say something like, "Sam, you are so good at praying with the kids at night. That's really a gift God's given you."
- Reminding him of God's presence, power, and promises. "Jim, I really think God is doing something good in you through this difficulty you're experiencing at work."
- Listening to him talk about himself. Let him tell you all about his day without being irritated that the subjects he dwells on seem shallow to you.

As we do these things for our husbands, we will feel God's pleasure and His love flowing through us.

Become convinced that you are the best person possible to minister to your husband's deepest needs. In fact, you have been handpicked for this job! And believe it or not, your extensive knowledge of your husband, *including those things that repel you*, make you the most qualified for and capable of the job.

Because you know your husband's most unlovable traits, you are more capable of bringing to bear love than any other human being.

Because you know what hurts or ails your husband better than anyone else on earth, you are God's greatest tool to bring healing and redemption to your husband's soul.

Because you know your husband's sins and failures better than anyone, you are by far in the greatest position to extend the forgiveness of Jesus and make it real to him.

Because you are keenly aware of your husband's needs, you can pray for him in a way no one else can.

Because you know the nature of his challenges and setbacks, you are in the greatest position to cheer him on, to encourage him to win in his life.

Your spouse may not notice that you are doing these things for him, but if you are doing them because you believe that God has called you to, then you will be given grace to continue. "Perhaps your spouse will not join you on the path to oneness," notes Crabb. "But you can maintain your commitment—first to obey God and to minister to your spouse through each opportunity that arises. The result will possibly (and in many cases probably) be a better marriage. The result will surely be a new level of spiritual maturity and fellowship with Christ for you."[3]

> *Dear Lord,*
> *What a wonderful challenge! It's so obvious, so basic*
> *to what it means to be a Christian and be married.*
> *Yet I miss it. How many opportunities to minister I've*
> *let pass me by. Forgive me. Change me. May I be*
> *more and more aware of how in serving my husband,*
> *I serve You. When I think about it that way—*
> *imagining that every sacrificial gift is also for You—*
> *suddenly, loving my husband seems so easy. Serving*
> *him sounds so easy—in spite of how hard it can be! I*
> *want this miracle, Lord. I believe that when a wife*
> *can see past her husband to her Lord, it is a miracle.*
> *Please help me ready my heart to receive it and to*
> *act on it. Amen.*

twenty

"She Did It...
Why Can't I?"

*I know that God is good to those who love Him. But
when I look at how some people seem to benefit from
sinning, I start to lose my footing on the truth...I say
to myself: Have I done the right thing by staying with
my husband for nothing? Are efforts to do the right
thing in vain? After all, I see other wives who leave
their husbands find happiness and blessings.*

A PARAPHRASE OF PSALM 73:2–3, 13

Almost every church has at least one couple like Peggy and
Dan in their midst. They've attended the church regularly
for ten years, but no one suspected they had any serious marriage
problems until Peggy announced that they were splitting. Neither
of them had had an affair. No one was being abused. But Peggy
wanted out. She felt miserable and lonely; she resented Dan's inability to express affection as well as his obsession with golf. She felt
like a single mom to their two kids.

After several years of trying to improve the marriage and seeing no progress, she decided that God was "giving her the grace to
leave."

Today, Peggy is remarried to a man we'll call Curtis. Together they share a blended family with four kids, her two and his two. And…here's the part that can be hard to reconcile: They seem so happy! Even their kids are doing remarkably well. "It all worked out. God is such a magnificent redeemer," says Peggy. "He forgives us and helps us start over when we fail."

If you know someone like Peggy, you've likely thought, *How can this be? I've tried to be a good Christian and do what God wants. I'm doing what I can to make this marriage work, and yet I'm miserable! How is it that God can allow her to be so happy when she got a divorce—just because she wasn't happy?*

Many of the biblical writers struggled with this same issue. Jeremiah did. He wrote:

You are always righteous, O LORD,
  when I bring a case before you.
Yet I would speak with you about your justice:
  Why does the way of the wicked prosper?
Why do all the faithless live at ease? (Jeremiah 12:1–2)

Habakkuk did. He wrote:

Why do you make me look at injustice?
  Why do you tolerate wrong?…
Therefore the law is paralyzed, and justice never prevails.
  (Habakkuk 1:3–4)

The psalmist also despaired, saying:

But as for me, my feet had almost slipped; I had nearly lost my foothold. For I envied the arrogant when I saw the prosperity of the wicked. This is what the wicked are like—always carefree, they increase in wealth. Surely in vain have I kept my heart pure; in vain have I washed my hands in innocence. (Psalm 73:2–3, 12–13)

Why do the rebellious prosper? Why should you try so hard to do the right thing if it's not making any difference? Is it in vain?

God's answer: "Do not let your heart envy sinners, but always be zealous for the fear of the LORD" (Proverbs 23:17). For wives in difficult marriages, God might say, "Don't envy wives who leave their unhappy marriages—even if they seem to prosper."

It's hard not to, though, isn't it? And why shouldn't we? The next verse makes it clear: "There is surely a future hope for you, and your hope will not be cut off" (v. 18). God assures us that regardless of what we think we see, there is more to be gained by doing the right thing than the wrong thing.

In his book *Celebrating the Wrath of God*, Jim McGuiggan offers this insight for those who wonder why good people suffer:

Naive solutions can injure, but there's something that injures even more—giving the impression that God exists primarily to keep us from being hurt. A faith that has more in common with cotton candy than with the biblical witness creates not only the need for so many overly-sweet explanations, it weakens our hearts and disables us.

While it's true that we don't have all the answers to the question of suffering, we do know what God has done in Christ, and Peter says if it's the will of God for us to suffer—so be it! If we're "gifted" with a difficult life as well as faith, we have God to thank (or blame) for it. "For it has been granted to you on behalf of Christ not only to believe on him, but also to suffer for him" (Philippians 1:29).[1]

Our choices matter for eternity. God forgives our sins, it's true. But He also promises to judge and reward each of us on the basis of our deeds. If we are only looking at a small slice in time, we won't see the big picture. If we are busy looking at others, whether they leave or stay, like the psalmist, we may lose our foothold (Psalm 73:2).

Besides, though it may look like a person hasn't experienced any negative consequences for their sins, he or she may be struggling more than you think. Peggy confesses, "I'll never stop feeling guilty about leaving Dan. I have this crushed feeling that intrudes on my happiness with Curtis. At the time, I was so numb, almost in shock at what I was doing. I didn't let myself feel. And then Curtis came along and suddenly I felt heady with romance. But after the romance wears off, you have a lot of the same old problems, only with a new guy. I envy those couples who don't have to split up their kids with exes, try to explain to them what happened, and for years, at every birthday, be reminded of their mistakes."

And here's something else to remember: For every Peggy there are five or six Jennifers. Jennifer got a divorce several years ago too. Close friends were aware that even though she accused her husband of failing to care about the marriage, she really wanted to pursue a flirtation with another man whom she insisted was just a friend. After the divorce, Jennifer and Just-a-Friend got together, and he became more than just a friend. For a while Jennifer was on cloud nine. It'd been so long since she'd been romanced, she felt her self-esteem rise and knew she'd done the right thing to leave.

Then, after a year, Just-a-Friend turned out to be not such a good friend. He'd never intended for Jennifer to assume they'd have a forever together. When she pushed for commitment, he found another lady friend. Today Jennifer is a single mom of three, despairs over her prospects, and wishes she'd never been so foolish to leave her husband, who by now has remarried.

But the Peggys and Jennifers of the world should not be our inspiration for staying in our marriages. Our primary motivation should be our commitment to God and our husbands—whether or not God grants our request for more happiness in our marriages. We can say what Habakkuk did when he realized that God wasn't going to answer his cries for help in the way that he had wanted:

> Though the fig tree does not bud
>> and there are no grapes on the vines,
> though the olive crop fails
>> and the fields produce no food,
> though there are no sheep in the pen
>> and no cattle in the stalls,
> yet I will rejoice in the LORD,
>> I will be joyful in God my Savior.
> The Sovereign LORD is my strength;
>> he makes my feet like the feet of a deer,
> he enables me to go on the heights. (Habakkuk 3:17–19)

While Peggy imagined God was giving her "the grace to leave," you are counting on God for the grace to stay. And your choice comes with guarantees: God's grace will sustain you. His grace is greater than any temptation. He alone can be your strength.

Yes, God is willing to redeem, forgive, and love the Peggys of the world. But how much more can He bless your marriage! No matter how miserable your marriage feels, in God's economy—in light of eternity and all that matters—you are always better off if you stay. Always! You might not see evidence of it today. You might not be able to grasp all you are being spared from because you stay. But it is real. "There is surely a future hope for you, and it will not be cut off."

Dear Lord,
You know my heart, and You know that sometimes I
am envious of other wives. Those whose marriages
seem easy and fulfilling. Those who appear to enjoy
the kind of happiness and family harmony that so
often escapes our family. Today I pray that by Your
miraculous power at work in me, I will be able to lay
aside all jealousy and envy. I want this marriage,
Lord! Help me to want it even more. Make me
content with what You have given me. Amen.

twenty-one

"Who... Me?"

*But He said to me, "My grace is enough for you,
because My power shows up best in weak people like
you." Therefore, we don't have to feel ashamed,
because we know that Christ's power can be
demonstrated in our weaknesses, and others will be
encouraged.*

A PARAPHRASE OF 2 CORINTHIANS 12:9

It isn't easy talking about pain, especially when it's ours. A lot of times we tuck in the ragged edges of our lives so no one will know the truth: We don't have it all together. There is great benefit in being real, being vulnerable, though. Did you ever consider that when we most need help and are in the most pain, we are in a prime position to minister to other women?

Romans 8:18 states, "Our present sufferings are not worth comparing with the glory that will be revealed in us."

We might wonder how any of our experiences could possibly "reveal glory" or benefit others, especially those who have witnessed our failures. But our faithfulness in loving our husbands and treating them with respect even when they continue to hurt us or disappoint us can be a testimony to others.

As Richard Foster points out in *Celebration of Discipline*, "The world is desperate and hungry for people who lay their lives down.

The fact that you hang in there does something for the rest of us Christians.

I'm not talking about inspiration. It's more than that. It's a mystery. God somehow strengthens others through your faithfulness. It's obvious—the power of God to transform your life is real and alive.

JONI EARECKSON TADA

Our world is hungry for genuinely changed people. Let us be among those who believe that the inner transformation of our lives is a goal worthy of our best effort."[1]

When you are in a not-so-perfect marriage, you may think you're the last one who should talk about marriage, much less teach or preach about it. But the opposite is true. Our pain is not meant just for us to endure and be comforted in. God can bring purpose out of our pain by using it to minister to others.

Second Corinthians 1:3–4 reminds us that it is "the God of all comfort, who comforts us in all our troubles, so that we can comfort those in any trouble with the comfort we ourselves have received from God."

I remember driving home from a Bible study one day, feeling totally defeated. My emotions had gotten the better of me. I had come completely unglued, a blubbering mess of raw pain. I glanced in the rearview mirror. Mascara tracks marked my cheeks; my eyes still looked swollen and red. I cringed, thinking of how I'd acted. I mean, it's one thing to ask for prayer, and even to cry softly while others gather around, praying and comforting you. It's another matter when an emotional dam bursts, leaving you vulnerable and helpless.

It had been a terrible morning. I had awakened to water gushing out of the downstairs shower, flooding the entire lower level of our house with ankle-deep water. All I could do was cry. Randy had been useless, still sleeping off a hangover. I managed to call a plumber, then forced myself out the door to Bible study. I knew it would help to have the group's support. I just hadn't expected to be so distraught.

Two days later, a card came in the mail from Linda, one of the women from the Bible study. "Deb, I'm so sorry for what you're going through," she wrote. "I just wanted you to know that you've given me a lot of courage. I'm having trouble in my marriage too, and I've been afraid to tell anyone. Thank you for being so real, so honest. Because of your faith, I believe there may be hope for us too."

Who...*me?* I couldn't believe I had encouraged anyone that day. God has a way of using us when we least expect it, though. He brings beauty even from the shambles of our lives.

So the next time you feel like the last person in the universe God could ever use, don't be surprised when you find out just the opposite. He wants to use you, and He already has someone in mind.

> *Dear God,*
> *I can't believe You could ever use me to help others.*
> *My life is such a mess. But I've heard You don't waste*
> *our pain. It can be used in Your beyond-my-ability-*
> *to-understand economy. Help me stay on the right*
> *road when I want to run the other way, when I don't*
> *want to deal with the pain, when I want to pretend*
> *everything is fine. Help me grow in my relationship*
> *with You, Lord. I pray for Your mercy and grace to*
> *help us in our time of need. Amen.*

twenty-two

Rethinking the S Word

*Wives, submit to your husbands as a way of
submitting to the Lord, and in the same way you'd do
it for the Lord.*

A PARAPHRASE OF EPHESIANS 5:22

Submission? C'mon, nobody really believes in that anymore, do they? Wasn't Paul just being patriarchal and chavin-
istic?

Actually he was being brilliant. Sometimes the key to turning a
huge corner in our marriage is so simple, so obvious, that we miss
it. Maybe you've heard all and more than you ever wanted to hear
about biblical submission. But have you really tried it? Really put it
to the test?

Ironically, even the secular world knows that submission
works! A recent book released in the general market called *The
Surrendered Wife* was an instant bestseller. Not because Christians
bought it, but because even non-Christians have discovered that
God's principles work—whether they give God credit or not. In
truth, the passages in the Bible about submission, whether written
by Peter, Paul, or Moses, aren't there just to make women frustrated or trip us up. God included them because they are power-

ful keys to unlocking joy and freedom in marriage.

So if submission is so great and works such wonders, why do so many of us wives resist it so heartily? There are several reasons.

We have the wrong idea of what it means to submit. True biblical submission doesn't mean giving your husband permission to abuse you or to treat you as inferior. Nor are you supposed to discount or nullify your feelings or opinions. Neither is it something weak women do (in fact, it takes great strength to surrender!).

Rather, submission in marriage is God's genius plan to help the two of you avoid irreconcilable conflicts and to make sure there's a place for the final buck to land. When a wife says, "When he starts loving me like Jesus loves the church, I'll start submitting to him like he's Jesus," she's missing the point. Ultimately, a wife submits to God when she submits to her husband.

True biblical submission comes out of a heart that says, "I trust God so much that I believe He will work through my husband to guide us, even if he doesn't seek His guidance. I will continue to ask him to honor my feelings and listen to my opinions, but I will no longer fight, punish, badger, or attack him when we disagree. I will no longer go behind his back against his wishes. I will no longer seethe with resentment when he makes a decision I don't like, or one that ends up being a bad one."

We are afraid of what will happen if we lose control. Submission is the opposite of one of our strongest impulses—the desire to be *in control*. Control allows us to feel safe from anyone taking advantage of us. We think, *If I truly let my husband lead, we'll end up in the ditch.* Or worse, *He'll take advantage of me terribly!*

While that is sometimes true, it's also true that when a wife truly submits, a husband is usually so thrilled with the respect she's giving to him, he's *more* likely to seek her opinions and advice.

"When I started to submit to Dale, there was an amazing change," shares one Nebraskan wife. "Before, when Dale and I were both fighting for control, both wanting the final say and to have things our way, he fought me tooth and nail. Dale is a CEO, a non-Christian, and arrogant to boot. I never felt heard. But now that I'm trying to submit and have even told him so, he's worried. People in business understand what it means to be the person where the buck stops. He feels the weight of the responsibility. Now Dale is including me, seeking my advice when I least expect him to. And because he no longer feels threatened by my input, he's much more likely to see something my way. It's amazing!"

We think two heads are better than one (and ours is the more spiritually discerning of the two). It's true that the best decisions are made when more than one person looks at the problem. However, if both have final say, then what? Imagine a country with two presidents.

Submission has nothing to do with giving up your right to contribute opinions, feelings, and even facts that inform the decision. It only has to do with the very real need for a final decision maker in moments of crisis or conflict.

Obviously, the glitch comes when a husband doesn't care what God thinks or wants. What if your husband asks you to do something contrary to Christian principles? In his book, *Experiencing Spiritual Breakthroughs,* Bruce Wilkinson points out:

> If Desperate Dan tells Edna Mae she must rob the corner market, she cannot obey his instructions. God said, "Do not steal." If Sleazy Sam tells Rosie to become a prostitute or to commit some other clearly immoral act, she is not free to obey his instructions. God said, "Do not commit adultery"

and gave other commandments concerning sexual behavior. The opportunity for the wife in these situations is to decline to do the wrong act because of her higher allegiance to God—without showing disrespect for the husband who is proposing it....

And what about situations that threaten the wife with violence or danger? The same principle holds true. A wife who is submitting to God can't cooperate with what the Bible describes as sin. Paul's picture for Timothy of the man who is worthy of being overseer is that he be "not violent, but gentle, not quarrelsome" (1 Timothy 3:3).[1]

If this sounds challenging, that's because it is! Submission never feels natural—it goes against our nature. You can make a decision to submit one day, and then the next day find yourself engaged with your man in a shoot-out for control again. Don't get discouraged! Keep at it. Turn your attempt to submit into an ongoing spiritual experiment and see what happens. Whenever one person in a marriage makes a dramatic change in how he responds to and treats the other, the relationship *always* changes. It has to. Try it and see if it doesn't make your marriage better and you happier.

Lord,

Wow. This is a tough one for me. I don't even like the word submission. Just the sound of it makes me rebel inside! Please, please turn my perspective around. Help me to change the way I view submission. Do a deep, inner work in my heart that banishes the lies about what it means to submit and sets my spirit free to submit in a loving, easy, willing way. A way that isn't about fear, insecurity, or weakness, but about strength and commitment and faith. I don't believe in my husband's ability to lead, Lord. But I believe in Your ability to work through him, no matter what. By Your grace and power at work in my heart, turn me into a woman who makes submission a priority and a joy. Amen.

twenty-three

Emotional Ping-Pong

Above all else, guard your heart, for it is the
wellspring of life. Don't let your emotions lead you
into speaking rashly or saying things about your
husband that you shouldn't. Keep your eyes open and
walk carefully, making wise decisions based on truth
and not on your feelings.

A PARAPHRASE OF PROVERBS 4:23-26

hen Sasha was in the midst of a recent crisis with her husband, she wished that she could shut off her emotions. "It'd be so easy to do all the things Jesus asks us to do, like forgive, love and honor your husband," she explains, "if we just didn't have emotions. That's where I fall down every time! My feelings never match up with what I want to do, whom I want to be."

A woman's ability to feel, to be emotional, is a beautiful gift from God, isn't it? Yet our emotions can make us prone to acting on our feelings instead of acting on what we believe or know to be true. For one thing, the sheer intensity of emotions like panic, shame, rejection, sadness, and anger can toss us around like a Ping-Pong ball in a hurricane. For another, most of us have been raised to honor our feelings as being more powerful and true than our choices. We've heard all the clichés: Follow your heart, we're told. Love made me do it. Can't help myself. But if we follow this kind of thinking, our strong feelings quickly turn into a blanket excuse for whatever we do next.

Any woman who chooses to stay in a tough relationship has to face her emotional ups and downs straight on. How can you do this?

Talk to God about your feelings. Larry Crabb points out that our emotions, both sinful and non-sinful—should prompt us to seek God's help. And when we do, we should do so honestly. He writes:

> Both sinful emotions (e.g., greed, lust) and non-sinful emotions (e.g., sorrow, grief, regret) need to be fully acknowledged before the Lord…. This does not consist of superficial prayers like "Oh, Lord, please forgive me for being angry." Rather, it is better to cry, "God, I am furious! I am livid with rage! And I know I am wrong! I want to go Your way and be filled with Your compassion, but right now I am bitter. Please forgive me! I commit myself to Your purposes." I am emphasizing that we must never suppress any emotion, whether by denying its existence or by minimizing its fullness.[1]

Determine to feel your emotions without acting them out in sinful ways. While some emotions are sinful, we can feel these same emotions and not sin. We can feel anger and yet not be controlled by our anger. But we can also feel hurt and lash out in sin. Paul wrote, "In your anger do not sin" (Ephesians 4:26).

For example, let's say you walk in the door after a long day at work and your husband, who's sitting on the couch with the kids says, "Oh no! Better change the channel, kids. Mommy doesn't like Jerry Springer. She only likes to watch religious nuts on TV."

Your blood is at a boiling point before he finishes speaking.

Your first inclination is to stomp over to the TV and turn it off, then start yelling at your husband right there in front of the kids. "How dare you make fun of my beliefs in front of our kids! How dare you let them watch this smut!"

The fact is, you have every right to be furious. But you don't have every right to lose your temper or start a yelling match with your husband in front of your kids. Both of these approaches are understandable, but not helpful. A better idea might be counting to ten before you say something or waiting until you've calmed down. Then ask the kids if they'd mind if you talked to Dad alone. Later you can explain to the kids that you and their dad have different ideas about what's right or wrong to watch on TV, and you're sorry they get caught in the middle.

Ask what your negative emotions might be trying to tell you. God made us to have emotions, and when we experience pain or rage or sadness, it's for a reason. Just as physical pain is an important indicator that something is amiss in our body, emotional pain can indicate that something in our spirit is crying out to be treated or healed. Likewise, recurring anger or rage may indicate we feel fundamentally violated in some way. Depression may flag us that we have been burying our anger rather than risking a conflict that might erupt if we release it. In this sense, our emotions are always valid and need to be acknowledged and owned by us. But we should ask: What is this strong emotion saying to me? Why do I feel this way, and how can I best address it?

Remember that while your emotions are part of a spiritual experience, they don't define truth. We can too easily mistake our feelings for God's will. For example, I've heard wives say that "God gave them a peace" about a decision to leave their marriages because they no longer loved their husbands and they believed that God wanted them to be happy. They used their feelings to justify their behavior. When we are in pain, it's critical to remember that our feelings are just feelings. They do not represent truth.

You can choose to treat your spouse in a loving manner, despite your feelings. What does this mean for those of us in challenging marriages? It means that even when we're feeling disappointed or hurt or angry, we can choose not to let those emotions determine how we behave toward our husbands.

Wendy, a mother of five, has an interesting policy. "When I am most angry or disappointed in Gary's behavior, I will make a list of the ways he's let me down. Then I burn the list, and I purposely do something kind for him for each thing on the list, like take out the trash (his job) or make his favorite dessert. He rarely notices when I do these things, but it doesn't matter because a big reason I do them is because when I act on the principle of love instead of my feelings, by the time I'm done, I often feel the love more than the negative emotion."

Gary Chapman writes:

> I am always influenced by my emotions, but I need not be controlled by them. This reality has profound implications for a troubled marriage. It means that I can do and say positive things to my spouse in spite of the fact that I have strong negative emotions. To take such positive action does not deny that our marriage is in serious trouble. It does not overlook the problems, but it chooses to take steps that hold potential for positive change rather than allowing negative behavior to escalate.[2]

By the power of the Holy Spirit, the truth of the Word, and the good counsel of His people, we can feel our feelings and yet not be controlled by them; we can make right choices regardless of how much we're hurting. We can let the fruits of God's nature, not the whims of our feelings, determine what we do and say. When we do, we will be making the most of the gift of our emotions.

And we will no longer feel like a Ping-Pong ball tossed about in a storm, but instead like a bird in a cleft of a hill, safe under God's covering.

> *Dear Lord,*
> *Thank You for the gift of emotions—for joy, empathy, and gratitude as well as pain, fear, and shame. I know that if I am walking with You, all of these feelings have a purpose and can be part of making me more and more like You. Help me not to be controlled by my emotions, but to be informed by them, to be fully human and yet not sin. Help me not just to react to what I feel, but to respond to it based on what I know as well. Give me the courage not to squelch or bury painful emotions, but to bring them to You and deal with them honestly and wisely.*
> *Amen.*

twenty-four

Sleeping with
the Enemy

*You have heard that it was said, "Love your neighbor
and hate your enemy." But I tell you: Love your
husband even when he acts like your enemy, and
pray for him when he opposes you.*

A PARAPHRASE OF MATTHEW 5:43–44

*I*f your husband intentionally does things to hurt you or
acts against you, you understand the ironic agony of the
phrase "sleeping with the enemy." Of course, you don't really consider your husband your enemy or you wouldn't be reading this
book. But "sleeping with" implies ultimate trust, surrender, intimacy, and vulnerability. The enemy is someone who acts against
you, who opposes you…. He certainly doesn't act as if he loves or
cherishes you.

When your husband behaves like your enemy, you feel
betrayed by the very person who should be your closest ally.

Mary Anne puts it this way: "My husband Josh continually
swears and uses four-letter words around our children even though
he knows how much it hurts me and how greatly it confuses the
kids. He tells them that just because Mommy's religious, they don't
have to believe in God. Sometimes when I'm crying and want to

talk something through, he just turns on the TV and raises the volume. I feel like he intentionally hurts me. With a husband like that, who needs enemies?"

The psalmist Davis understood the pain that comes from being betrayed by a dear friend. Listen to him describe his experience:

> Fear and trembling have beset me;
>> horror has overwhelmed me.
> I said, "Oh, that I had the wings of a dove!
>> I would fly away and be at rest—
> I would flee far away
>> and stay in the desert;
> I would hurry to my place of shelter,
>> far from the tempest and storm."
> If an enemy were insulting me,
>> I could endure it;
> If a foe were raising himself against me,
>> I could hide from him.
> But it is you...my companion, my close friend,
>> with whom I once enjoyed sweet fellowship.
> (Psalm 55:5–8, 12–14)

We can see David's emotional profile at this moment: he is fearful, shaken, overwhelmed, urgently wishing to run away, and deeply shocked and hurt. He's tempted to run—in fact, he did run—for his life. And sometimes wives have to do the same.

In the movie *Sleeping With the Enemy*, Julia Roberts plays a young wife whose husband turns from nice to nasty. Violence and fear become a way of life for her until she flees the marriage to try to start over in another town, living under an assumed name.

In some situations, we need to run as fast as we can from an enemy. If your husband is violent with you or your children, you should flee. No exceptions. No spiritual justification for endangering you or your kids' welfare. (See appendix, question 1).

Of course, a wife can still feel in conflict with and deeply hurt by her husband, even when he's never hit her or their kids. At such times, the hard gospel of Jesus can sound impossible. He said,

> Love your enemies, do good to those who hate you, bless those who curse you, pray for those who mistreat you. Do not judge, and you will not be judged. Do not condemn, and you will not be condemned. Forgive, and you will be forgiven. Give, and it will be given to you. A good measure, pressed down, shaken together and running over, will be poured into your lap. (Luke 6:27–28, 37–38)

For those whose husbands are their biggest source of pain, these words suggest a seemingly impossible response. How do we bless a husband who curses us? How do we repay evil with good?

But there is a way through. Jesus knew that apart from the power of God, His gospel was impossible for ordinary people in tough situations. But with the power of the Holy Spirit, out of our weakness can come the kind of giving and forgiving that will change us and those we love.

In her book *Blessing Your Enemies, Forgiving Your Friends,* Kristen Johnson Ingram tells a powerful story of how a friend's choice to bless her enemy changed many lives:

> My friend Leta was assaulted while walking home from work at sundown. Despite her screams, the attacker covered her mouth, threw her onto the lawn behind the hedge, and raped her. He then fled into the dark.

Eventually, people heard her screams and came to her aid. But it was too late. Leta had been attacked in mind, body, and emotions; she wanted to die.

Leta's pastor, as well as personnel from the local rape crisis center, tried to help her immediate hurt and rage. But Leta was emotionally damaged, almost defeated. She quit her job, broke her engagement to the man she loved, and went back to her hometown. For months she hid in the bedroom of her parents' home, refusing to see her fiancé or old friends. Finally, expecting to hear comforting words, Leta allowed a nun from her home parish to visit her. She was shocked to hear Sister Patricia say, "Leta, I want you to bless that man!"

Leta ordered the nun to leave and retreated to her room. Sister Patricia, however, left behind a handwritten reference to Luke 6. Although Leta read the note and threw it away, she couldn't get the nun's voice out of her head. Again and again, she heard the command, "Bless that man!"

After several sleepless nights and difficult days, Leta sat on the edge of her bed with her fists clenched. She whispered, "God bless the man that raped me…."

Leta didn't feel like blessing her attacker, but in the spirit of obedience, she said the words. At dinner that night, she noticed her appetite was better than it had been for months. Connecting that slight improvement with her prayer, she uttered another prayer of blessing for her attacker. Within a few days, Leta called Sister Patricia and made an appointment to see her. It was the first time Leta had been out of the house in three weeks.

When the rapist was captured and brought to trial for

several counts of rape, Leta testified against him. Rather than demanding revenge, however, Leta asked the judge to send the man where he would get help, so he could redeem his life. To her rapist, Leta said, "I will pray for you."

Today, Leta is married to her longtime sweetheart and works at a women's counseling center, where she is known as "Bless-'em-all Leta." The man who raped her is in a prison sex-offender program. Leta prays for him every day.

More than one life was redeemed in this process: Leta's, her rapist's, her distraught parents', and her fiancé's. "One word changed me from an angry, depressed victim into a victorious woman of God," Leta says. "The word was *bless.*"[1]

Maybe you can relate to Leta's initial reaction: "Bless my enemy? Are you kidding?"

That reaction may be understandable, but you can choose to bless your husband. Like Leta, you can pray for God to bless him. You can forgive him every day for his offenses against you. You can do something kind for him—rub his shoulders while he watches TV, for example—in spite of the fact that he has treated you rudely all night.

Melinda, whose husband Bob is "very demanding" and hostile toward Christianity, makes a point of giving a verbal blessing to her husband every morning as he goes off to work. She's discovered that by simply leaving out the word *God*, Bob welcomes her encouraging words: "May you be blessed with a peaceful day, Bob." Or "May you be blessed with a creative breakthrough today."

As you set out to bless your husband, keep in mind that it should always feel good to you to bless your husband. If not, check your motives. You don't bless him because he's earned it. You bless him because of a radical decision on your part to reverse the dynamics of opposition or hostility your husband may be introducing into your home and marriage.

Many days in a not-so-perfect marriage bring opportunities to run, to hate, to retaliate…or to reach for the impossible by God's power—to give and forgive without thinking of what's fair, to withhold judgment when evil has been done, to do good when none will be returned, and to ask for God's most abundant blessings for the husband who has acted as an enemy.

> *Dear Lord,*
> *What You ask of me is so opposite my natural*
> *impulse! When my husband feels like my enemy, I'm*
> *afraid the last thing I usually do is bless him or pray*
> *for him. The good news is that now I see how I can*
> *make a dramatic change! One that, if I succeed, will*
> *transform my entire outlook. Please give me Your*
> *extraordinary power and grace. I cannot do this*
> *alone. But with Your help, I will try. Amen.*

twenty-five

Sex Matters

*I have already gotten settled in bed, wearing my
flannel nightgown and reading my book. Now that
you're in the mood, I'm not sure I want to go to all
the trouble....*

A PARAPHRASE OF SONG OF SONGS 5:3, 6

ometimes the well-worn excuse, "I've got a headache,
honey," is actually true. Just the thought of having sex makes
your head hurt, and maybe your heart as well. It's hard to feel
amorous when you're angry or disappointed, and it's equally difficult to desire your husband sexually if you're not attracted to him.

Many women in difficult marriages lack a desire for sexual intimacy with their mates—and you don't have to look far to understand why, at least in part. We're all aware that women are wired
differently than men when it comes to sex. While men are aroused
by visual and physical stimuli, women usually need to feel affection
and trust in order to be responsive to a man's sexual advances. When
a wife receives her husband during intercourse, she is, in a sense,
allowing herself to be invaded by him—not just physically, but on
emotional and spiritual levels, as well. Wives who feel loved and
secure welcome this invasion as an opportunity to experience

intense intimacy and pleasure with their husbands. But wives who lack sexual desire or who feel animosity toward their husbands often experience sex as a violation rather than as loving communion.

Many women in difficult marriages find sex undesirable. So, if you have problems in this area, know that you're in good company—and that you can take steps to have a more satisfying and healthy sexual relationship with your husband.

You may be surprised to learn that Scripture can shed some insight into why you may be feeling resistant or resentful when it comes to lovemaking. In a well-known but often misrepresented passage about marriage, Paul writes: "The husband should fulfill his marital duty to his wife, and likewise the wife to her husband. The wife's body does not belong to her alone but also to her husband. In the same way, the husband's body does not belong to him alone but also to his wife" (1 Corinthians 7:3–4).

These verses have been used to browbeat wives into feeling guilty for not wanting to have sex or for avoiding it. But notice that Paul doesn't say a wife's body belongs *only* to her spouse. It says it belongs *also* to her spouse. As "one flesh," a wife shares her body with her husband. Bible commentaries also point out that when Paul says we "belong" to one another, he's not just emphasizing our ownership rights over one another, but he's also clarifying that our exclusive conjugal rights belong to each other—no outsiders allowed.

This passage does not teach that a wife (or husband, for that matter) should submit to sex whenever, wherever, and however our partner demands it, no matter how we feel. Rather, it teaches that since my husband's body belongs to me, I should care about it enough to give it pleasure whenever I possibly can, and he likewise with my body. In the same way, since my husband's body belongs to me, I should also be understanding and generous when it's not "in the mood," and he likewise with my body. The emphasis is on mutuality, not on selfishness.

At first reading, this passage may also seem to teach that sex is a duty, a required act. But duty is better translated as *sacred responsibility*. Paul is advising couples to continue to have sex on a regular basis because sex is at the heart of our sacred oneness and helps to protect our fidelity. The intent of this duty isn't that a wife complies with a husband's selfish appetite for sex on demand or vice versa, but to fulfill her sacred obligation to meet her husband's sexual needs, keep the marriage bed pure, and keep each other free of sexual temptation.

Let's look at another passage. In Ephesians, husbands are told to love their wives "as their own bodies" (Ephesians 5:28). "After all, no one ever hated his own body," Paul writes, "but he feeds and cares for it, just as Christ does the church" (v. 29). God describes a husband who loves his wife so much that he puts her needs as high on the chart as his own bodily needs! In regard to sex then, if a husband loves his wife this way, there's no danger that he'll mistreat her or take sexual advantage of her, because that would be like hating his own body.

In God's ideal picture of marriage, if a wife wasn't feeling up to sex, for whatever reason, the husband would honor and respect her feelings as if it were he himself who wasn't in the mood. If a husband *doesn't* love his wife this way, he—not she—is sinning when he expects his wife to be available for intercourse on demand and without regard to her feelings.

Okay, so now we see that God didn't intend for a wife to be a slave to her husband's sexual needs. However, the other extreme—saying that a wife has no responsibility or can shirk her obligation to nurture a healthy, ongoing sexual relationship—is equally wrong and unbiblical. A wife who regularly refuses to have sex or is only willing to be intimate with her husband on her terms is also acting selfishly. If you consistently rebuff your husband's sexual advances and resent intercourse, you need to take active, positive steps toward restoring consistent and mutually satisfying lovemaking to your marriage.

Here are some suggestions to start you on the path to discovery and change. For starters:

Tell your husband that you want to improve your lovemaking and you are actively pursuing positive changes. Assure him that you understand that you have a part in the sexual problems in your marriage. Be sure he knows that your goal is for both of you to be sexually satisfied.

Take a "time out" from sex. Paul said not to deny each other except for a time of prayer (1 Corinthians 7:5). The reason for a sexual hiatus isn't to avoid sex—it's to pray and to take active steps to bring about change. It's not to stop resentment from building, it's to bring healing so that resentment is no longer an issue. Talk about this with your husband. Tell him what you're doing and why. If he knows the goal isn't less sex, but more and better sex, he'll likely feel less threatened by a time out and be more willing to see a counselor together, read books together, or otherwise explore the problem. If he gets angry or refuses to respect your wishes, talk with a counselor in order to gain wisdom and support for what you can do.

Educate yourself. There's not enough room here to address the myriad emotional and physical aspects of sexual dysfunction, and there are plenty of good books available. One or both of you may have grown up with ideas or teachings about sex that are inhibiting you now. Some good Christian books include:

- *Restoring the Pleasure* by Clifford L. Penner and Joyce J. Penner
- *Intimate Issues* by Linda Dillow and Lorraine Pintus
- *Intended for Pleasure* by Ed Wheat

Check your history. Could it be that past sexual relationships are interfering in your present one? Were you involved in sexual activities earlier in life that left you feeling resentful and used? If you have a history of any kind of abuse, chances are great that you need healing from these hurtful experiences before you will begin to have a healthy attitude about lovemaking. Since this is a complex issue, you should seek help from a professional as soon as possible.

Rule out physical problems. Sometimes physical problems, such as hormone imbalances, inhibit a woman's desire for sex. If your troubles have more to do with a lack of physical responsiveness than with emotional resistance, see a physician who specializes in sexual dysfunction and explore possible causes and solutions. You should also visit your doctor if you don't experience orgasms, if you lack lubrication, if you find intercourse painful, or if you are on medications that might be interfering with your sexual drive.

Experiment with being the initiator. In most cases where a wife is reluctant to have sex, the husband is the designated initiator, which can lead to an unhelpful pattern in which the problem only gets worse. Authors Clifford and Joyce Penner point out:

> Because the wife does not show her interest in being together sexually, the husband begins to believe she has no interest in him sexually. His insecurity is triggered by her apparent lack of interest, so he anxiously begins to initiate sex more often than he would want it if he were feeling sure of himself in relation to her. She feels pressured by his initiation, so she begins to avoid him or pull away sexually. The more he approaches, the more consistent is her avoidance. The more frequent her avoidance, the more anxious is his approach. It becomes a negative spiral.[1]

Talk with your husband about waiting for sex until you approach him. Many men, once assured that sex will take place, aren't put off at all by waiting for the wives to signal their readiness. If you are the initiator it may remove some of the feelings of pressure and duty you experience. Instead, it becomes something you are giving, versus something he is always approaching you to take.

Spell it out for him! "If she [a wife] feels uncared for, she may believe the only interest her husband has in her is sex," write the Penners. "He comes home from work, turns on the television, sits quietly at dinner, and watches television after dinner. Then at bedtime, he becomes friendly—and her anger sizzles."[2]

Sound familiar? Tell your husband exactly what it takes to please you in bed and to make you feel happy to be invited there. You'd be amazed how many men just don't realize that a wife needs to be courted during the day, instead of only five minutes before lovemaking. And chances are, it probably doesn't take that much: a midday phone call, kisses on the way out the door, a long hug when he gets home. Be specific about what you'd enjoy and list for him several small things he could do to help you be in the mood more often.

Consider sexual therapy. For some couples, the road to a healthy sex life may require outside help. Often sexual therapy involves literally starting all over again with a clean slate. Couples typically follow a program that begins with nonsexual touching; over the course of weeks, homework assignments build back up to intercourse (*Restoring the Pleasure* contains a step-by-step program). If your husband is unwilling to see a counselor with you, consider seeking help alone. You'd be surprised how much progress you can make this way. A therapist may not only be able to help you deal with your own issues pertaining to sex, but may also help you find nonthreatening ways to talk about them with your husband.

Be honest about turnoffs. It's important to find a way to let your husband know what dampens your mood. For years, Catherine's husband Jason had no idea that his wife was repelled by the smell of a prescription lotion. When she finally mentioned it one night, he was hurt that she'd never been honest before. Now he never applies his bedtime dose of lotion until he's sure that they won't be making love.

If it's something he can change, let your husband know that while you accept and love him as he is, you'd think he were sexier if he could deal with this particular problem. If it's not something he can change, the problem then becomes yours. In truth, your sexual responsiveness to your husband, if all else is well, shouldn't be dampened by baldness, graying, or wrinkled skin. If they trouble you, you need to deal with your own thought patterns and values and try not to let them detract from lovemaking.

Making changes in your sex life won't necessarily come easily. Some changes might not come at all. However, never give up or relegate sex to the old days. A healthy sex life is foundational to every marriage. The Penners put it this way: "How important is sex in marriage? A simple answer is that when sex is compared to an automobile, sex is to the marriage what oil is to the combustion engine. At least a little oil is necessary to keep the engine running— without sex, one's marriage will eventually break down."[3]

> *Dear Lord,*
> *Thank You for the gift of sex! I want to become more*
> *and more grateful for this miracle of oneness You*
> *created. Help me, I pray, to do everything in my*
> *power to make my love life with the husband You*
> *gave me all that You would have it be. Restore our*
> *passion, revive our affections, and fill us with mercy*
> *and grace for one another. Amen.*

VOICES: KENDRA'S STORY

Like most couples, Kendra and her husband Artie enjoyed lovemaking immensely during their early years of marriage. But after Kendra gave birth to two boys two years apart, the frequency of their sexual relations dramatically declined. Kendra didn't think Artie minded much. But could it be that their flagging sex life was at the root of a host of other marital troubles they were having?

When Artie and I were first married, we had a great sex life. Then came two kids two years apart. After I had kids, it felt like someone came along and just sucked any sexuality I had right out of my body. To be honest, my "Not tonight, honey" turned into "Not this week, honey." When things began to fall apart in other areas of our marriage, I began to worry that if something didn't change soon, I'd be saying to Artie, "Not in this lifetime, bucko!"

I had no idea marriage would be so hard and motherhood so draining. The last thing I wanted at the end of the day was a man making demands on my body. Whenever Artie approached me with that look in his eye, I tried to act like I didn't notice. I made sure our kisses were just smooches or pecks. I began to avoid wearing attractive nightgowns, thinking that this would help him not think about having sex (I was still naive enough to imagine an hour went by when a man didn't think of sex).

Our lack of lovemaking wasn't something we argued or even talked about. Artie just backed off.

Kendra's Story

When our marriage continued to spiral, the last thing I would have traced our problems to was our infrequent lovemaking. It seemed like our main problems had to do with Artie and his immaturity. First he quit going to church, and then he was beginning to hang out with his old crowd from high school. He checked out as a dad, and it seemed like he just wanted to stay twenty forever.

Meanwhile, I began to feel more and more like a single mom. My whole world revolved around doctor's appointments, preschool, grocery shopping, and housecleaning. And I completely lost sight of why Artie and I were in all this together in the first place: Oh yeah, we were supposedly so deeply in love that we wanted to spend the rest of our lives together. What a joke!

Finally the fighting and arguing about his lack of help around the house and his frequent nights out got so bad we decided to go to counseling. It was either that or just give up. We'd even begun using the *D* word.

After several weeks of telling a Christian therapist everything we hated about each other and why we were so miserable, the counselor asked us about our sex life. Artie blushed and I played with my purse strap. "Uh…yeah…sex?" mumbled Artie. "Yeah, we have sex. Not enough, but once in a while."

That admission turned out to be the opening the therapist was looking for. He insisted that we got onto a regular program—a schedule!—of lovemaking. I was pretty certain I'd fallen victim to the whims of yet another dumb male. Couldn't this man see that we didn't need better sex, but a better marriage? But since this was the first thing the counselor suggested that Artie seemed to respond to (I should say, seized upon), I begrudgingly agreed to try it.

It was hard, uncomfortable. Just like I knew it would be. I think even Artie found it awkward that first week. Not knowing how to go about initiating something, he'd make a joke of it and say, "Hey, babe, tonight's the night. Doctor's orders."

At the next session I challenged our therapist: "Why should I make love when I'm not in the mood? Won't that just make me resent Artie more?"

He said, "As long as you see it as something you give to him to reward good behavior, yes, it will. Do you tell Artie what feels good and what doesn't? Do you both take it slow and try to pleasure each other? Lovemaking does not have to mean intercourse, by the way.

"And Artie," he continued, now directing his attention to my husband, "do you treat Kendra all day long in a way that leads naturally to lovemaking?"

Artie agreed he could try harder to show me affection during the day. I admitted I'd never really told him what I like in that department and promised to try.

So we kept at it. I prayed about it a lot, even if Artie didn't. Over the next few months, we began to make slow progress. Gradually, sex began to shift from something I saw as my duty to something I welcomed. I learned to resist the little lie that said, You're too tired tonight. You have a headache, remember? Instead, I reminded myself that once we got going, once I was aroused, it would be good. And afterward I'd sleep even better than if we hadn't made love.

One night Artie told me, "You seem like my lover again, not just a mom." And I realized it was true. Things had changed some. He'd been spending a lot more time with me and the kids and going out less.

With the rebirth of our sex life came a subtle rebirth in our marriage. All our problems didn't go away. But somehow, with that vital connection in place, we were reminded of the basics—that we are, first of all, lovers. And yes, we were in love. I've decided I'm in this marriage for the long haul. And I think Artie has too. Now I joke with him that if he does ever leave me, it had better not be for lack of sex!

twenty-six

Too Busy to Believe

When we take time out from our busyness to be
quiet, then we have an opportunity to know God.

A PARAPHRASE OF PSALM 46:10

*I*f the devil can't make you bad, he'll make you busy, or so the saying goes.

I'm sure you've been there. Christmas is on the way: preholiday panic is overwhelming. A stack of packages wait to be mailed, boxes of unwritten Christmas cards also beg attention. The calendar overflows with activities: the church's caroling party, school programs, your child's school Christmas party (you're bringing the treats), the usual carpooling commitments, and maybe a neighborhood cookie exchange, if you can work it in.

And you haven't even started your holiday baking. Of course, you want at least a dozen kinds of cookies—not old standards like chocolate chip and oatmeal, but jam-filled tea cookies, frosted gingerbread men....

After one such crazy Christmas, I recognized that my life had become a whirlwind—not only during the holidays, but every day. I couldn't stop running. My endless lists, places to go, and people to see took every moment. I raced through each frantic day. I rationalized that what I was doing was God's work—helping others, volunteering at school and church. Yet I felt burned out and frustrated.

I determined to change. I told myself, "I'm going to slow down. With the Lord's help and some time management tapes, surely I can get my schedule under control!" But gradually, in spite of my good intentions, the harried routine took over again.

I think God almost has to hit some of us with a two-by-four to get our attention—at least He does me! It took falling on an icy sidewalk while I ran from one event to the next, fracturing my kneecap, and being sent to the couch to recuperate for several weeks for me to face reality. It was as if the Lord had put up a giant stop sign that I had slammed into. I had to sit still whether I liked it or not. I was a "busy addict," forced to stop cold turkey.

The up side: Four knee surgeries later, after months of quiet recuperation, I had come to grips with what lay beneath my drive to stay busy. The truth startled me. I wasn't busy because I had to be, because I was indispensable, or because I was just an overly good and helpful person. I was crazy-busy because I wanted to be. While I complained about my busyness, deep down, the more I jammed into each day, the better I felt.

There were two reasons for this. One was my need to feel affirmed and significant. I equated busyness with feeling important and needed—qualities lacking in my marriage. Since I couldn't fix Randy, I took care of everyone else, substituting their affirmation for the support Randy couldn't give me. My security wasn't found in my relationship with God (as I had thought), but in striving and achieving, trying to please others.

Second, and maybe more obvious, busyness enabled me to avoid my marriage problems and the pain I felt about them. If I was lost in a blur of activity, then I didn't have time to dwell on the fact that Randy was drinking more than ever. By attending to what I thought were worthy causes, I could ignore my growing resentment and pain. And the adrenaline high I got as I dashed from one

> We must learn to rest in God and completely trust Him for our own sense of well-being and 'place' in this world.
>
> WILLIAM BACKUS

place to another medicated the lonely ache I felt inside.

After my knee recovered, I tried a different approach. I made it a point to allow myself to feel my pain and then to take it to God. The pain didn't necessarily go away, but I was finally in a position to receive God's comfort. And it was—is—real and wonderful! How much better is God's comfort than the tactics of avoiding or anesthetizing, which are no comfort at all. I also found better ways to cope with feelings of insignificance. I made adjustments in how and why I decided to "do for others." And then I put some of that freed-up time and energy to work, focusing on improving my troubled marriage.

Let's face it. All of us are busy. And lots of us wives in difficult marriages tend to get too busy. Maybe for you it's work that keeps you frantic. You put in overtime, try to be the office hero. My friend Sally says she can't help being busy, since she has four kids to homeschool. That's okay! It's important to note that busyness in and of itself isn't bad. Maybe your schedule involves a lot of good things. You try to prioritize. The point is to be sure you aren't staying busy for the wrong reasons: to make up for what's lacking in your difficult marriage or to avoid feeling the pain of your marriage.

Like me, you may know or suspect the truth about your busyness but feel afraid to stop and be still. Here's something to try: Make a list of all the things that keep you busy. But instead of prioritizing each item, ask yourself, what is my true motivation for doing this? It's a revealing exercise that can help you move toward

God's plans and purposes for your life instead of signing up for every worthy cause that comes along.

Jesus consistently took time away from the crowds who clamored after Him in order to be refreshed, to pray, to hear from the Father. We need to do the same. Try journaling your thoughts as prayers, take a walk away from the city's hectic pace if you can, or listen to soothing sounds of praise music while driving, especially in rush-hour traffic. Better yet, find a quiet, comfortable place at home where you can meditate on the Bible, allowing it to nurture your soul.

When we take time to be quiet, we are more likely to draw near to the Father, to read His word, pray, and listen for His guidance and direction. Is the Lord trying to tell you something about how you relate to your husband? Is He speaking to you about your attitude? Are there changes you could make in your schedule to create more balance at home? When you are still, you are more likely to find answers to these questions.

Jesus said, "Come to me, all you who are weary and burdened, and I will give you rest" (Matthew 11:28). Today He invites you to run to Him, not from your reality. He invites you to be still, to be honest, to hear his voice. And, one might add, to find your place in a challenging marriage.

> Dear God,
> I'm tired of trying to do it all—in my own strength. I realize I've found my value in what I do, not in who I am in Your eyes. I need rest. I come to You and place my burdens, fears, anger, and resentments in Your hands. I believe You will guide me and help me find healing so I can stop running away and run to You instead. Amen.

twenty-seven

The Most Crushing Blow

With persuasive words she led my husband astray;
she seduced him with her smooth talk. All at once he
followed her like an ox going to the slaughter, like a
deer stepping into a noose.

A PARAPHRASE OF PROVERBS 7:21–22

We've talked about your vulnerability to an affair. But what if your equally vulnerable husband falls prey to one?

Proverbs speaks at length about the perils of adultery for a man who strays. Over and over again, the writer warns of dire, painful consequences. But when a man walks into the noose of an affair, the wife is equally snared and wounded.

Pam remembers how inconsolable her best friend was when she discovered that her husband of ten years had been unfaithful. "I don't think I will ever forget the guttural sounds she made when she showed up at my doorstep having just had her worst fears realized," says Pam. "I've heard a lot of tears, but none has ever sounded like hers did that day. In my head I think I silently called her husband everything in the book of bad words I could think of—even as I tried to rapidly work through how I would help her fight for her marriage when I wanted to kill her husband myself."

No chapter in a book can adequately address the painful issues a wife faces when her husband strays. It's a complex issue; every incidence of adultery is different. However, one key to coping with any affair, be it yours or a friend's, is understanding what motivated the husband's unfaithfulness. Because there are so many kinds and degrees of sexual betrayal, the path to recovery and the prospects for the marriage are largely determined by what led to the affair in the first place.

A husband's infidelity usually falls into one of these three categories:

Crisis-motivated adultery. A husband may sleep with another woman because he's struggling with his own identity or the direction his life has taken. This husband may love his wife, but he feels trapped, suffocated, and without options. As self-destructive as it sounds—and is—having an affair is one way to force a crisis. When the affair comes to light, often this husband can't explain why he did what he did. He's usually repentant; in fact, he often breaks the news of the infidelity to his wife himself, or he gets caught on purpose. Counselors agree that there's hope for this marriage to last if the husband gets the help he needs in order to understand and resolve the underlying issues that led to his affair.

Sexually-motivated adultery. This is the guy who visits the prostitute while on a business trip or who can't resist the sexual advances of his secretary—or any other attractive female who makes herself available. His main motivation is sexual gratification. Often, this husband also struggles with pornography. He tends to be highly secretive and filled with shame about his activities. If he will agree to get help and become accountable to someone—in addition to his wife—this marriage also has hope for a better relationship. If he's deeply addicted to his sexual lusts, this couple may have a long, hard road ahead, but if they will travel it together, they're destined for a stronger marriage.

Emotionally-motivated adultery. By far the most devastating affairs are those in which a man believes he has fallen in love with another woman. This is true for two reasons. First, when a husband is unfaithful in both heart and body, his betrayal is complete. The wife must deal not only with her husband's sexual infidelity, but also with the transference of his affections to another woman. In many cases, the husband has experienced with her the kind of intimacy and romantic love that the wife herself has longed for. Second, this husband may not even want to save his marriage. Unless dramatic measures are taken to keep the two people having the affair from any further contact, there's a chance that the affair will drag on, if not physically, emotionally.

If the husband ends the affair and wants to save the marriage, it can survive and even improve. But the road ahead won't be easy. The painful fallout from this kind of an affair is often felt for years to come.

Chances are that as you read through these descriptions you were able to pinpoint the kind of affair your husband is most vulnerable to (and that you can help him be on guard against). If he's already been unfaithful, you were probably able to identify the category that best describes what might have motivated his actions. This insight can help you know better how to pray for him, and it can help both of you decide what kind of help you should seek.

However, we still haven't addressed a key question that applies to adultery of all kinds: What if your husband continues in an affair or is chronically unfaithful?

As you're probably aware, unfaithfulness is the one condition God cites as an acceptable reason to seek a divorce (Matthew 19:9). But just because you have biblical grounds for divorce, it *doesn't* necessarily mean your marriage has no hope or will end in divorce. However, it also doesn't mean that you should suffer your husband's ongoing infidelity in silence. If your husband is caught up in an affair or you suspect he is being unfaithful, here are some general guidelines to keep in mind:

- You shouldn't be expected to continue having sexual relations with a husband who is actively sexually unfaithful. The writer of Hebrews says that the "marriage bed should be kept pure" (Hebrews 13:4).
- You shouldn't allow yourself to be humiliated by letting your husband receive phone calls or be contacted in any way by a lover.
- If your husband has had an affair—even if it is a one-time event—get yourself (and him, if he's willing) examined by a doctor to test for sexually transmitted diseases.
- A habitually unfaithful husband is an abusive husband. He is attacking the very foundation of your union together, which is why the Bible allows for divorce in such cases. Treat a chronically unfaithful spouse in the same way you might treat a physically abusive spouse. Leave, or have him leave your home. Seek help and counsel from a qualified third party and refuse to reconcile until your husband has met a certain set of criteria that you and your pastor or counselor have developed together. For more on separation, see chapter 35.
- Remember, even if your husband pleads again and again for mercy, he expects you to lay down some basic boundaries. If you don't, he will respect you even less than he did in the moment when he betrayed you, and it's very unlikely he'll change his behavior.
- If the relationship is volatile, avoid being alone in his presence

and consider communicating through a third party. Never contact the "other woman." As satisfying or as reasonable as the idea might sound, such confrontations rarely improve a situation and often exacerbate it.

- If your husband refuses to end an affair and yet doesn't seek or want a divorce, you will have a difficult choice to make. After separating and getting plenty of counsel, decide how long you are willing to wait for your husband, if at all. Then let him know in clear terms what you've decided.

- Don't file for divorce or make life-changing decisions when you are in a state of emotional upheaval. Wait until you are able to think clearly and calmly.

As you consider your options, keep in mind that many husbands discover down the road that the other woman isn't what they really want, after all. Because God has been known to do miracles in even the most devastated marriages, keep that possibility in mind.

When your husband has been unfaithful, whether he stays or leaves, the last thing you want to hear about is forgiveness. And that's natural. Understandable. But sooner or later, you will have to deal with the issue. There is no neutral ground. You either forgive or you don't. And in the case of a marriage devastated by an affair, the difference between the two will grow more and more apparent as the years go by.

You are at a pivotal point. Many couples find that an affair is a wake-up call that in the end saves the marriage because it brings to light some deep, underlying problems and forces the couple to deal with them. Sometimes the house has to crumble before it can be rebuilt the right way, piece by piece.

The path to forgiveness is a difficult, painful one. But as you'll see in the next few pages, it's also full of promise. And you never have to walk it alone.

> *Dear Lord,*
> *You alone can fathom the depths of pain that I feel about my husband's infidelity. It feels like someone is shelling the walls of my soul. It feels like someone is scraping me clean inside like a pumpkin. Give me hope, God. Give me something to hang on to when I feel like I can't go on. Give me wisdom and patience during this critical time in my marriage. Everything is on the line. And I am so weak and broken. I cast myself and my marriage upon You, Lord. And I beg for Your divine, saving intervention. Amen.*

twenty-eight

Impossible Forgiveness

*Be patient with your husband, and forgive him the
same way that the Lord forgives you.*

A PARAPHRASE OF COLOSSIANS 3:13

Few stories in the Bible arouse our curiosity more than the story of Hosea and Gomer. Chapter 3 of the book of Hosea opens with this surprising verse: "The LORD said to me, 'Go, show your love to your wife again, though she is loved by another and is an adulteress. Love her as the LORD loves the Israelites'" (Hosea 3:1).

God asked the prophet Hosea to show love to his wayward wife in order to illustrate His love for His people. But one has to wonder: How many of us would not only take back but show love to a straying spouse?

Adultery is by far the hardest thing to forgive in a marriage. But Hosea and Gomer's story illustrates a point that goes beyond just forgiving adultery. It is a picture of how we can forgive all kinds of grievous sins against us in the same radical way God forgives us— freely and unreservedly. Even when they least deserve it.

How hard this can be to do! Especially when we know our anger and hurt are legitimate, that we're in the right and our mate is in the wrong. Or, for that matter, when he doesn't even seem sorry for what he did.

When Shelly discovered her husband Rick had a one-night fling on a business trip, he said he was sorry, but he didn't really seem to feel the kind of pain or grief over his sin that she'd hoped for. "I could tell he didn't really grasp how much he hurt me," explains Shelly. "I stayed in bed and cried for days on end. But Rick, though he'd say the right things so far as how sorry he was, didn't seem to feel much of anything. Somehow, over the next six months, I found a way to forgive him anyway. Fully. Freely. One night, I was being kind to him, kissing his ear, and he suddenly broke down. He sobbed like a baby for half an hour, begging my forgiveness. He said my love in the face of my pain was what finally broke through his hard heart."

There are no limits to the forgiveness God asks us to grant to others. But there are limits on what forgiveness is and what it implies. Often we struggle to forgive because we have wrong ideas about what forgiveness means. Not just in our heads, but deep in our soul.

We imagine that when we forgive someone, we are condoning, denying, or ignoring the offense. God didn't ask Hosea to bring his wife home and just do nothing while she continued to be unfaithful. Just the opposite! God wanted to use Hosea's response toward his unfaithful wife to show Israel how deeply compassionate He was toward her. But He wanted Israel to return to Him and become faithful as well. Hosea didn't tell Gomer, "It's just fine that you did this to me. No problem." Instead, when he forgave Gomer, he also put his foot down. "Then I told her, 'You are to live with me many days; you must not be a prostitute or be intimate with any man, and I will live with you'" (Hosea 3:3). Note that the point of Hosea's story is *not* that a spouse should stay with a partner who continues in adultery. Forgiveness puts its foot down in love, refusing to tolerate continued offense.

Jesus too models this. He encountered a woman just like Gomer some five hundred years later. She was about to be stoned for her adultery when Jesus shamed her accusers, forgave her, and then told her to "go now and leave your life of sin" (John 8:11).

Jesus' forgiveness of those who killed Him did not negate the depth of their evil or what they had done to Him. Their sin wasn't cancelled or ignored or dismissed. It was fully recognized, counted as sin—and forgiven! And that is why His forgiveness was so powerful. The same is true when we forgive in the same way.

We imagine that when God asks us to forgive, He wants to gloss over our wounds and pain. Picture yourself as a little girl who's been attacked by a bully on the playground. You're lying on the ground bleeding, and God comes by and says, "Hey, there. You look hurt. Did you forgive the guy that did that to you?"

No wonder we clutch our wounds so tightly.

But the truth is that God cares deeply and is angry on our behalf when we are hurt. The prophet Malachi explained to the Israelites why God was no longer accepting their offerings with pleasure: "You ask, 'Why?' It is because the LORD is acting as the witness between you and the wife of your youth, because you have broken faith with her, though she is your partner, the wife of your marriage covenant" (Malachi 2:14).

God is also "acting as the witness" in your marriage. When your husband deeply wounds you, God takes up your cause. When He asks you to forgive, He is not asking you to say it doesn't matter that your husband hurt you, but to choose not to take revenge yourself. He wants you to be so confident in His love for you and His perfect justice that you're willing to leave vengeance to Him.

Consider Romans 12:19–21: "Do not take revenge, my friends, but leave room for God's wrath, for it is written: 'It is mine to avenge; I will repay,' says the Lord. On the contrary: 'If your enemy is hungry, feed him; if he is thirsty, give him something to drink. In doing this, you will heap burning coals on his head.' Do not be overcome by evil, but overcome evil with good."

This is not to say that we forgive, all the while thinking, "Just you wait! You'll get yours!" But we don't have to spend time worrying about vengeance at all, since God is just and we can trust Him. Once we choose to forgive, often we stop *wanting* that person to be judged or pay a price. We move past saying, "I choose to forgive my husband, Father. You take care of this," to actually withdrawing our rights to God's vengeance and saying, as Jesus did, "Father, forgive them."

We imagine that forgiving is forgetting rather than redeeming. Sometimes what happens after we grant forgiveness to our mate is as important as our original choice to forgive. Hosea had to live with the legacy of Gomer's adultery—illegitimate children, gossip in town, feelings of hurt and betrayal. And Gomer had to live with the shameful knowledge of what she'd done.

Even when we forgive our mate for a lesser offense than adultery, we often share the heartache of the consequences. A week later, when we're still paying a price somehow, it's tempting to say, "I forgive you—but look how much your mistake has cost us!"

Especially when our mate has deeply hurt us, forgiveness is only the first step on the road to redemption. Not only might the offended mate have to pay some price (in Hosea 3:2 we learn that Hosea had to pay financially as well as emotionally), but the person who has been forgiven must accept lingering consequences, such as his mate's hurt feelings or nagging distrust.

So how can the seed of forgiveness blossom into full redemption? By cooperating with God to turn this offense into good.

Christ is our inspiration and our help at such times. Not only did He pay the price for our sins with His death, He committed himself to walking with us through the broken glass of all our mistakes. To go beyond forgiveness to redemption means asking, "How have we both been at fault? What can we learn from this?"

Sometimes as we're facing painful consequences or reminders, it helps to do something that will act as a symbol of the redemption we're claiming. When God relented toward Israel, He told Hosea to "show love" to Gomer. And then He changed the names He'd given Hosea's sons: "I will say to those called 'Not my people,' 'You are my people'" (Hosea 2:23).

For us, "showing love" to our husbands may simply mean that we agree never to mention a certain incident again. Or it might mean something more concrete, such as sharing a romantic dinner on the very same rug that we had a huge fight about buying.

Our human nature makes it so easy for us to cling to bitterness rather than to pursue healing. Yet by the amazing life of Christ, we have everything we need to start over after deep hurts—His hope, courage, humility, and understanding.

> *Dear God,*
> *I know that while I was "yet a sinner" Jesus died for*
> *me. This is the gift of undeserved forgiveness that,*
> *with Christ's help, I can also give my mate. And soon*
> *I'll discover that the price of redemption is worth the*
> *reward it brings. Thank You for Your help as I learn*
> *more about forgiveness and wait for Your continual*
> *redemption. Amen.*

twenty-nine

Angels

*Praise be to the God and Father of our Lord Jesus
Christ, the Father of compassion and the God of all
comfort, who comforts us when we are hurting about
our husbands, so that we can comfort others who
hurt with the comfort we have received from God.*

A PARAPHRASE OF 2 CORINTHIANS 1:3–4

God still sends angels: ones with skin, hair, and belly laughs. Angels like Jim. I met him at an Alcoholics Anonymous meeting where I was one of the speakers for Al-Anon. I was supposed to offer encouragement and hope for others who had alcoholic friends or family members.

I stepped up to the microphone, my heart pounding. I wasn't an experienced speaker; why had I said yes? Besides, Randy had slid deeper into the depths of his addiction. How could I talk about hope when I didn't have any myself?

Somehow I managed to say words that came from my heart. I didn't pretend to be okay. I simply told my story, unable to suppress my pain and grief.

A man wearing a baseball cap, hands shoved into his pockets, ambled up to me after I finished. Laugh lines marked his tan face. "I liked what you had to say. You know, Randy's story is like mine."

He pulled a business card out of his pocket. "If I can ever help you or Randy, please call me."

And I did. So began a friendship only God could have orchestrated. Jim lived an hour from us, a ferry ride across Puget Sound from our Seattle suburb. He was always a phone call away, always ready to listen to Randy or me, always ready to offer support, and even some humor.

One night I dialed Jim's by-now-familiar number. "Jim, I'm having company tonight, and Randy's drunk. He's asleep on the bedroom floor. What should I do?" I spewed out my anger and hurt.

Jim calmly advised, "Can you just cover him with a blanket, close the bedroom door, and go on with the evening?"

I hadn't even considered that. I'd been frantically thinking of ways to contact everyone, cancel the event, and then seethe with resentment.

"I know you can do it," Jim said in a fatherly tone.

And I did. The evening came off without a hitch. No one knew my husband slept upstairs in an alcoholic stupor. I had a good time—and even managed to forget our problems for a while.

As I continued to use Jim as a lifeline, he would often say to me, "Randy needs compassion." Jim frequently quoted from Jesus' Sermon on the Mount or from 1 Corinthians 13. I squirmed when he talked about love.

"I can't love Randy," I protested. "I don't like him at all today. In fact, I just might hate him."

Jim patiently listened, then gently reminded me that Randy was a child of God. Jesus had died for him too. He recounted his own struggles with alcohol and his ability to identify with Randy.

When Randy lost his job, Jim came across the water to comfort us. We three knelt together in our living room on that bleak

November day, asking for God's grace and mercy. Jim reassured us life would get better if Randy could only surrender to God. *He needs your love,* Jim's eyes pleaded. Reluctantly I became willing to love even when I felt nothing. My heart was moved with compassion for my husband, and I began to see him as a man thoroughly broken and defeated by his addiction.

People like Jim are more than friends…angels, perhaps? His compassion had helped to penetrate the coldness of my heart, my inability to love. Only God could come up with such a plan, just the right person at the right time to help us. Jim had earned the right to be heard. He had suffered the consequences of bondage to alcohol. And he had gained much wisdom from his encounter with pain.

You can do the same thing. God wants to use the painful challenges you face today to comfort someone else down the line. It's part of His wonderful plan of redemption. He sends you comfort, and then you pass it on, with an extra scoop of wisdom added on top, to someone else who is in need.

Today, watch for angels God sends your way. And remember that you, too, are an angel in the making.

> *Thank You, God, for sending people to help us just when we need them, reminders of Your promise to never leave us alone or forsake us. When we're hurting, help us remember that You have a way of using our suffering to comfort others. Our pain is never wasted in Your economy. Amen.*

thirty

"I'm So Lonely!"

Right now, be graciously real and present to me,
Lord. For in spite of being married, I am so lonely
and so sad.

A Paraphrase of Psalm 25:16

One of the hardest aspects of being in a difficult marriage is the loneliness. A wife may have many friends, be active and busy, and even surrounded by people who need and love her. But if she's in a seemingly loveless or empty marriage, the inner loneliness can be overwhelming. "It's like drowning, only on the inside," says Marta.

Another wife puts it this way: "My marriage is the relationship that *should* offer me the most intimacy imaginable. But instead it leaves me feeling rejected and estranged. When you're part of a whole and half is missing, you walk around with this raw edge of hurt inside that you can't seem to fix."

Often, the loneliness we feel in a not-so-perfect marriage has nothing to do with our husband's proximity. He may be home at six o'clock every night but miles away in his heart. Amy feels that way about her husband of twelve years, Calvin. "The first five years were great," she says. "But then we just began to drift apart. In the muddle of kids and appointments and work and what's for dinner...we lost each other. One night I was lying in my bed journaling to God, trying to gain a sense of peace. Calvin climbed into bed next to me, and I realized with shock that his physical presence—so near and yet so distant—actually made me feel terribly alone. It felt like an intruder was climbing into bed next to me."

How do you cope with this kind of deep loneliness? There are no easy answers. But there are some steps you can take to stem the tide of sadness.

Make sure your husband knows you're lonely. That might sound elementary, but we often communicate our loneliness in ways our mate doesn't even hear. Jan, a pastor's wife from Oklahoma, tells about a time when she was in the kitchen making dinner, feeling sorry for herself. Her husband seemed so wrapped up in his church that he didn't seem to notice her anymore. She'd tried to talk to him about his priorities, about his long hours...and he kept promising it would get better. But it hadn't. "Then that night as I was loading the dishwasher, something hit me," Jan says. "I realized I'd never really looked Gary in the eye and said, 'Gary, I'm so lonely.' After I finished in the kitchen, I found him in his den. I didn't make any demands. Or rebuke him for his schedule. I just told him flat out, 'I'm lonely,' and left it there.

"His response was amazingly caring. It felt like the first time he'd really heard me. That night before bed, we talked. Finally. Heart-to-heart. It'd been so long since we'd discussed *me*—my dreams, my fears, my needs—in a way that reached beyond Jan the mom, Jan the wife.... This time we actually talked about Jan. The Jan that still exists down inside, the Jan who wants and needs to be connected, intimate, dreaming alongside someone. It was a breakthrough.

"Then, a few weeks later," she continues, " I noticed that Gary seemed quiet, kind of down. He was spending a lot of time puttering in the garage, in the attic. Heavy sighs. I asked about his work.

He said it was okay. Later that night as I was offering to help our daughter with a time-consuming project, Gary came up to me and said, 'Can I tell you something? I'm lonely.' Now those two words have become a key, a signal we send each other when our souls are lonely despite physical proximity."

Of course, not every wife will get the response Jan did from Gary. Even if you tell your husband you're lonely, he might only hear it as an accusation or complaint. He might move further away. Then what?

Keep in mind that your loneliness may not be entirely about your husband. In other words, while it's true that you feel alone in your marriage, other factors may be causing you to feel this way. Sometimes what you really need might be solitude, to literally *be* alone. Solitude is not the same as loneliness. Solitude happens when you choose to be alone on purpose. Solitude gives you a chance to refill your spiritual reserves. Use that time to get back in touch with yourself and with God. When your "well" is full, your husband is more likely to be drawn to you. If you come to him empty, trying to get him to fill your needs, he's likely to run in the opposite direction.

Jesus understood the value of solitude. We read in Luke, "Yet the news about him spread all the more, so that crowds of people came to hear him and to be healed of their sicknesses. But Jesus often withdrew to lonely places" (Luke 5:15–16). Maybe you can relate to that feeling of everyone clamoring for your attention: your kids, your job, your husband. You look anything but lonely, but you are. Jesus was seeking connection. Even though He was the Son of God, He still needed to be deeply connected to His Father. Are there lonely places you can retreat to where you'll meet your Father?

Be aware that your loneliness makes you vulnerable. It is perhaps the most dangerous feeling of all in a marriage. Loneliness is like a clarion call that your spirit begins to sing. And like a bird call-ing for a mate, in time there's a good chance that someone with that song is bound to hear and respond. He will present himself as the answer to your loneliness. He will look—and act—like the exact solution. He will seem to be a shape that fits perfectly into the empty shape inside your soul.

Of course, this is a deception. Only the cross will fill that empty place. But all this is not to say you don't need your husband's near-ness. Denying how much loneliness hurts is not the answer. Neither is deciding that you will learn not to care or that you don't need him. Close friends certainly can and do help alleviate our loneliness. But there's danger in using friends and activities to assuage our loneliness to the point where we don't feel our need for our husband anymore. That need for him is a *must* if your marriage is to survive. It hurts to feel that need. It hurts to long for his near-ness and not have it. However, canceling it out will cancel out hope that you and your husband could draw closer and make the rela-tionship more satisfying. Leave the door to your heart open, even if it looks like he'll never come walking through.

> *Thank You, God, that I am not alone. When I truly*
> *need someone, You are like a husband to me—*
> *comforting me and blessing me with Your nearness.*
> *In my loneliest moments, help me to come to You, to*
> *seek You. Thank You for helping me see that*
> *loneliness can be a gift that brings grace in the most*
> *unexpected ways and places. Amen.*

thirty-one

Getting a Life

See! The winter is past; the rains are over and gone.
Flowers appear on the earth; the season of singing
has come. Forget your troubles and spend some time
enjoying the life God gave you.

A PARAPHRASE OF SONG OF SONGS 2:11–12

I left the house early on an August morning while Randy slept. I'd smelled alcohol on his breath the night before, and though I wanted to confront him, I knew better. He would just deny that he'd been drinking. It wasn't worth the energy. Instead, I decided to drive to Seattle.

I boarded a ferry to one of the islands and enjoyed what turned out to be an almost perfect day. The sparkling clear sky formed a magnificent backdrop for Mt. Rainier. Sunshine warmed me as I sat on the deck, breathing in the fresh, salty air. I had lunch with a friend, wandered in and out of quaint shops, and picked a glorious bouquet of flowers at a dahlia farm. I forgot to be angry. In fact, I forgot all about our problems. I returned home feeling refreshed and energized. Then it hit me! I'd had a good day even though Randy was still drinking.

For much of my life, my emotions typically held me captive. Negative thinking paralyzed me. *What am I going to do? What if he doesn't ever stop drinking? What if I always feel this miserable?* What if this, what if that.... I thought up endless lists of potential disasters, many of which never even happened. But then a counselor commented, "Why are you spending so much time in the future, Deb? You're worried so much about what might happen that you don't ever have any fun. You need more fun in your life." She was right. I had become so focused on Randy I didn't even know what it meant to do something I enjoyed anymore. My identity as a person had gotten blurred.

Nowadays, I try to do things that are good for me, that remind me of who I am and what's important to me. I try to get a good night's rest, eat sensibly, and have regular mealtimes, and I take time to exercise. Basic, yes, but while I was obsessed with changing Randy, I rarely slept well, had difficulty maintaining a consistent schedule, and rarely had the energy to exercise. Now I enjoy outdoor recreation such as hiking, cross-country skiing, and snowshoeing. (I even bought myself a pair of snowshoes with some gift money. In the past I would have felt guilty purchasing an impractical gift. Today I see it as a blessing!)

I also try to take some time for myself each day. Some mornings I snuggle on the couch to read the Bible and pray while appreciating the early morning quiet. On other days I enjoy my alone time after work. My dog Kramer and I walk through fields by my house down to the Chewuch River. We play fetch and other fun doggie games on each trek. Fun is an important part of my life now!

Randy and I like to watch movies (especially comedies), and we enjoy family times with our sons when they visit. We usually end up playing cards or board games long into the night. A women's Bible study, playing piano for worship at church, and a cup of tea with a good friend all bring me joy. How far I've come since that enlightening day spent on Bainbridge Island so many years ago.

> The most powerful and positive impact we can have on other people is accomplished by taking responsibility for ourselves and allowing others to be responsible for themselves.
>
> MELODY BEATTIE

At first you might feel uncomfortable doing things simply because you enjoy them. It seems selfish to think about yourself, about not always putting others' needs before your own. Certainly, as Christians, we are commanded to love our neighbors, to treat others with kindness and compassion. But sometimes we forget the other half of this command—"as ourselves."

Richard Foster writes in *Celebration of Discipline:* "If we think we will have joy only by praying and singing psalms, we will be disillusioned. But if we fill our lives with simple good things and constantly thank God for them, we will know joy."[1]

Joy begins today. Each day is a gift. Now, this moment, is really all we have. Taking care of yourself means starting in small ways to enjoy each day.

What renews your spirit and gives you joy? Do one of those things today—and another tomorrow. Watch the sunrise, sip a cup of tea while reading God's Word, write a letter to or e-mail a special friend, buy yourself a flower, look for the Big Dipper in the night sky, bake your favorite recipe for cookies and give a dozen away. Don't forget to laugh, keep your sense of humor, lighten up! Try something new such as painting, writing, gardening. Enroll in a class, get a job, change careers. Go to a support group; try counseling, even if by yourself. Volunteer your time and talents.

A friend once said, "I honor the Creator when I honor His

creation—and part of His creation includes me!" When we do things that nurture and comfort us, that revive our spirits and brighten our outlook, we will break out of a victim mentality. We can find joy each day—we just have to look for it in the right place!

Dear God,
I need to get a life! I've lost mine somewhere along the way, trying to change my husband and our marriage. I've forgotten what I enjoy, the possibility that You have uniquely created me to do something for Your kingdom. What is it, Lord? I don't want to miss any opportunities to serve You. Help me find balance in loving others—and loving myself. I praise You, Heavenly Father, for the wonders You so graciously bring into each day. I don't want to miss any! Amen.

VOICES: DARLENE'S STORY

Darlene and Jim have been married for twenty-three years. There was a time when Darlene was fixated on the way Jim's job made him unavailable as a husband and father. He worked a swing shift and refused to change his schedule. She felt like he was purposely avoiding all the parenting responsibilities. Today, Darlene often works the swing shift at her full-time job but still finds time to enjoy gardening, tea with friends, and spending time with her best friend, Jim.

When our son Todd was a baby, Jim took a job that required him to work swing shift. This routine worked well for a few years because his schedule allowed me to attend some college classes in the mornings while Jim took care of the baby. Jim was paid more for working swing, and both of us enjoyed the extra income.

But when Todd started school, Jim began to see less and less of him, and I felt a growing resentment. I wanted him to be like other husbands who were home in the evenings. I felt increasingly alone as a parent. I asked Jim if he'd consider changing shifts. He refused, saying that we needed the money.

I was angry at his intransigence, and my resentment grew. I continued to state my case, saying that our son needed more time with him, but Jim continued to hold firm to his decision to work swing shift. Finally, when Todd was in the sixth grade, I realized that Jim had no intention of changing shifts. He said no, not to make my life miserable, but because he believed it was best for his career—and ultimately for our family. That day I cried out to God, "How can I be both parents and take on all this responsibility alone? My marriage—in fact, my whole life—feels too heavy for me."

God told me very clearly, "Darlene, your marriage, your unhappiness, your parenting concerns—everything that is your problem is my problem too. Why won't you let Me carry some of that?"

Of course, I'd heard that God cares about us and our problems, but that was the first time I ever felt it personally. What a relief! God could give me the wisdom and strength that I needed. I didn't have to figure out how to discipline and nurture Todd in a vacuum! I prayed and asked God to forgive me for trying to control Jim and to come to my aid as a parent. I told Him that I knew He had our best interests at heart, even if I couldn't see the end result.

And with God's help, I chose to be happy in this marriage. When I stopped complaining about Jim and feeling sorry for myself, I began to see that I had contributed to the unhappiness in our marriage—our problems weren't all Jim's doing. I stopped focusing on him and everything else I couldn't change and turned my attention to the only thing I could change: me.

I began to see that I needed to stop trying to "do it all"—laundry, cooking, grocery shopping, housework—and make parenting my priority. I asked God to give me wisdom, and He did.

I started to keep a daily consistent schedule. I planned sit-down dinners for Todd and me instead of meals on the run. I kept to a routine of housework and bedtime. I attended school and sports events and tried not to deprive our son of his parents' attention, just because his dad wasn't available.

I encouraged phone calls between Jim and Todd each day after school so they could still have a relationship. When we encountered discipline problems, if necessary, I called Jim and we handled the situation right then. He supported me and followed up with Todd as soon as possible. I made a point to plan special family times when we all had time off together on the weekends.

Jim never did change his shift, even though he noticed the changes in me. And when I stopped harping at him to change shifts, our marriage became a lot more peaceful. These days, Jim and I are the best of friends. My circumstances didn't change, but my attitude certainly did.

thirty-two

Emotional Baggage

When I was in a lot of pain, I finally asked the Lord
for help and He set me free.

A Paraphrase of Psalm 118:5

You could've heard a pin drop in Mrs. Miller's third grade classroom that September morning. Humidity hung like a heavy cloud. Students hunched over their desks, pencils scratching busily on paper tablets. I was the only one not writing. The black-rimmed clock ticked away the seconds until lunch. Panic gripped me. I didn't know any answers on the math test. My hands felt sticky on the Formica desktop, and sweat trickled down my back.

The boy in front of me slammed his book shut with satisfaction. Soon others followed. "We're finished," they seemed to jeer. The harder I tried to figure out the story problems, the more confused and afraid I felt. I wanted to hide, but I couldn't escape Mrs. Miller's piercing glare.

"Mrs. Miller," I said timidly, "I don't understand my arithmetic."

"What don't you understand?" she asked.

How could I explain? All I knew was that I didn't get it. Her exasperated look made me wish I could crawl in a hole somewhere.

She stalked over to my desk, hands on her hips. Beads of per-spiration glistened on her forehead. "Now—what don't you under-stand?"

"My arithmetic?" I whimpered.

Her hands clamped onto my shoulders. She shook me as if to force out the right answer. "What don't you understand?" she shrieked.

I felt frozen with fear. My tears dripped on the blank paper.

"Stop those crocodile tears," she demanded. All I could think of was getting out of there. "You're stupid," she pronounced. "Why don't you go home for lunch? We'll work on this later."

I raced down the rickety stairs and pedaled my bike home in record time. I could barely see through my tears. My breath came in short gasps as I told my mom what happened.

Forty years ago teachers were unquestioned authorities. Today Mrs. Miller would have been called on the carpet for her abuse of kids. But the mindset was different then. Mom comforted me, but I'm sure Mrs. Miller was never confronted or questioned for her behavior. All weekend I planned out ways to gain my teacher's approval. After all, this was only September and I had a whole school year ahead of me. I wanted her to like me. Shame and embarrassment gnawed at my tender self-image.

I found Mom's tin box of buttons, beads, and shiny sequins, and spent hours stringing colorful beads for the necklace I proudly presented to Mrs. Miller on Monday morning, along with a poem I'd written.

She hugged me. No trace of anger remained. She read my poem and a smile tugged at the corners of her mouth. "Deb, you're the smartest little girl I know—and the nicest too."

I beamed. I'd found the magic. If I was very good and didn't cause any problems, then I'd stay out of trouble and be liked by everyone. I'd especially avoid Mrs. Miller's unpredictable temper.

Sadly, it took me years to realize I didn't have to be afraid of going to school. I didn't have to cry about not understanding math. It was okay to make mistakes.

Obviously I don't blame Mrs. Miller for all my relationship problems. Yet I learned some coping techniques from her that served me well as a child but crippled me as an adult: Smile. Be nice. Don't rock the boat. Make sure everyone likes you.

We all have childhood stories to tell of someone's unwitting or purposeful wounding of our spirits. I've heard it said that "hurt people...hurt people." Our parents, teachers, siblings are imperfect. They make mistakes at our expense. Just as we have also affected our own children, students, and neighborhood kids by our behavior.

We refer to these accumulated hurts and learned responses as emotional baggage. Have you ever been late arriving at the airport for a departing flight? You promise yourself you'll pack lighter next time. You juggle your carry-on bag while hauling your overstuffed suitcase, which won't stay upright on its wheels. Your way-too-heavy purse hangs off your shoulder. Your back and neck already hurt. You're tempted to stop at the massage bar to get the crick out, but you're late!

Many of us come into marriage carrying baggage from our past—old hurts along with the deeply ingrained patterns of coping they've evoked. Often, these experiences, even more than the present circumstances, determine our patterns of relating with others. If you haven't forgiven your father for abandoning you as a child, for example, it may be getting in the way of your being able to forgive your husband. Or maybe your husband always clams up at the first sign of conflict between the two of you because this was how he learned to cope with his shrieking mother when he was growing up.

We cannot tell what may happen to us in the strange medley of life. But we can decide what happens in us—how we can take it, what we do with it—and that is what really counts in the end.

JOSEPH FORT NEWTON

If you or your mate have some emotional baggage, both of you probably feel frustrated and exhausted from trying to play a particular role that is no longer healthy.

How can we know if we have this kind of baggage? Sometimes we discover it with the help of a caring therapist or within a group of supportive friends. Sometimes we hear someone else telling about her own experiences. A lightbulb of recognition goes on in our minds. "That's me. I'm tired of hurting, falling into the same pitfalls. I want to be free."

If you suspect you are carrying some baggage from the past, don't focus your energy on looking inward or on blaming others for what happened to you. Instead, take responsibility for your actions today:

- Prayerfully ask the Lord to show you areas where you've been wounded by others' actions.
- Admit to the Lord how you really feel about what happened— i.e., anger, fear, shame, embarrassment.
- Ask God to reveal to you how the past is affecting the way you relate to others, how you respond to conflict, or how you communicate. Ask Him to help you change any patterns that are negatively affecting your relationships with others.
- Pray for the Lord to help you forgive those who have hurt you.

If you have trouble dealing with past baggage, be sure to seek help from a trusted pastor or counselor.

Remember, this isn't an overnight process. Old wounds take time to heal, and if you've been relying on certain behavioral patterns for many years, they are deeply ingrained by now. With prayer, perseverance, and determination, however, you can let go of more and more baggage from the past. And one day you'll realize you only have one carry-on bag, and it fits neatly under your seat.

Dear Lord,
I can't forgive anyone by myself. Your priceless gift of forgiveness for my sins is a continual reminder and example of my need to offer others forgiveness. Help me be aware of the ways I've been truly hurt. Unjust actions have wounded me, and I'm discovering how I've compensated. I've carried the burden way too long and I'm ready to let it go. Continue to reveal to me where the past is tripping up my present. You have given me a way to be free, to relinquish my bitterness and resentment. Thank You, Lord. Amen.

thirty-three

Choosing Obedience

*We know that we have come to know Christ if we
obey His commands. The wife who says, "I know
Him," but does not do what He commands is a liar,
and the truth is not in her. But if a wife obeys His
Word, God's love is truly made complete in her. This
is how we know we're in Him: Whoever claims to
live in Him must walk as Jesus did.*

A PARAPHRASE OF 1 JOHN 2:3–6

'm troubled by your attitude," my friend Pam told me gently but matter-of-factly. I had followed her outside after she excused herself from the Bible study her husband led in their home. I had an inkling that her distraction had something to do with my attitude about Randy's latest lapse. I was right.

"Just last week you were telling us how God had spoken to you about your anger and the way you treat Randy when he drinks," she said. "You were so determined to obey God in this area. Now you're telling all of us how you're going to go home and sleep on the couch tonight."

What she said was true. God had clearly told me to stop punishing Randy for his relapses, to stop yelling at him or giving him the cold shoulder. I'd been determined to obey God in this—until

Randy came home drunk again. "You don't understand what it's like!" I yelled at Pam. "Your husband isn't a drunk." I proceeded to vent my anger and frustration.

"You're right," she said. "I don't know what you've gone through. I can't imagine how hard it's been." She listened patiently to my anger until it finally ebbed into sobs of grief. Then she held me and allowed me to weep.

After my tears had been spent, I knew I had a choice. I could go home and verbally berate and reject Randy as usual, or I could do what God had told me to do at this juncture in our marriage: look past the drinking and love him.

Sometimes it's hard to obey God, especially when you've been hurt, betrayed, or treated unjustly by your husband. In fact, just the idea that God would ask you to obey Him in something, when it's your husband who is so out of line in your mind, can seem outrageous. Even the word *obey* sounds old-fashioned in light of modern, recovery-related language, doesn't it?

But God does demand our obedience. And this is good news, not bad.

When we obey God, we give Him permission and room to do miracles in our marriages. Sometimes we may not even understand what He's up to. He may ask us to do something that doesn't seem fair or appropriate. Yet He alone sees the big picture of our marriages, and so we can rest assured that He's qualified to call the shots.

Joni Eareckson Tada, a person well qualified to talk about obedience reminds us of yet another reason to obey. She writes, "When we hang in there, remaining faithful and doing good, our obedience deeply moves and pleases the God of the universe: 'For with such sacrifices God is pleased' (Hebrews 13:16)."[1]

So often we forget that we actually have the power to effect a

❦

Let me conduct myself and my life in such a way that I will have no reason to reproach myself for making a bad situation worse.

This, at least, is within my power: to make it better.

ONE DAY AT A TIME IN AL-ANON

response in God toward us. When we obey, He feels pleasure with us. But there's more. Did you notice the word *sacrifice* in the above Scripture? God understands that it hurts us to obey! He knows we'll have to give up something that costs us. For me, it was my right to be angry with and to punish my husband. How hard that was to let go! But how comforting to know that God sees our sacrifice in such situations—and is pleased.

When we obey God, we have our eyes on eternity. We obey because we believe that no matter what our circumstances, good will ultimately come from them.

Obedience involves both action and direction. Only when we actively choose to be a servant, to obey God's directives in our lives, can Jesus take His place as Lord of our lives. When we obey God, we redeem impossible situations simply because we bring God glory through our obedience.

I'm grateful for Pam's convicting words that day; they pierced my heart. With tears in my eyes, I told her that she was right. I asked God to forgive me for once again trying to control Randy and to give me the strength to love Randy as He wanted me to love him.

Dear God,

Forgive me for turning away from You, for stubbornly wanting my way, wanting to punish my husband when it isn't my place to do so. You've called me to love him, even when he doesn't "deserve" it. I am humbled when I remember that all of us fall short of Your glory. None of us deserve Your love. Yet You never turn us away when we come seeking forgiveness. Thank You for loving us most when we deserve it least. Thank You for Your grace, which is sufficient for me. Amen.

thirty-four

"I Was Wrong"

*Finally, all of you, live in harmony with your
husbands and be at peace with them. Be sympathetic,
loving, compassionate, and humble. When your
husband offends you, don't just automatically offend
him in return, even though you are in the right.
Don't insult him when he insults you. Instead, bless
him. Keep pursuing ways to make peace.*

A PARAPHRASE OF I PETER 3:8–9

recent cartoon in the *New Yorker* depicts a husband and wife who have obviously been arguing. The woman has her hands on her hips and is saying, "If it doesn't matter who's right and who's wrong, then why don't *I* be right and *you* be wrong?"

We chuckle because it's so true! For most of us, it really does matter who's right and who's wrong. We're deeply concerned about it—especially if we're in a challenging marriage. The hardest thing to say when we're in the heat of a verbal squabble or subsequent apology is "I was wrong." It's as if our mouths are stuck with peanut butter: "I waaaaas wrooooong..."

It's so much easier to say sorry, especially if we can just say, "Sorry you got your feelings hurt." This way we're still not necessarily wrong—the other person was just probably oversensitive or misunderstood us.

How often a poorly-put apology leads to yet another offense and more arguing! We all know what it's like to receive an apology that doesn't deliver because it's mixed with accusation or excuses. "I'm sorry that you saw it that way…" or "I'm sorry I yelled, but if you hadn't…"

In the book of Hosea, the prophet actually gives the people advice on how to apologize to God. "Take words with you and return to the LORD. Say to him: 'Forgive all our sins and receive us graciously, that we may offer the fruit of our lips. Assyria cannot save us; we will not mount war-horses. We will never again say "Our gods" to what our own hands have made'" (Hosea 14:2–3).

If we have to tell people what to say when they apologize, it may feel insincere. But if we don't, how will they know? A good apology contains certain key elements, all of which can be found in Hosea's advice to the Israelites. The next time you need to apologize to your husband, try these steps. You can memorize them thinking of the Four A's. If your husband is open and willing, you might tell him about them.

Admission: "I was wrong!" Even if you were not the only one who was wrong, own your part in the misunderstanding or offense.

Affirmation: "I understand that you feel angry and hurt." We all like to know that we've been heard, and that our reaction is understood.

Apologize: "I'm sorry I did that. I am going to try not to make this mistake again." A commitment to change or to try to avoid the offense in the future reaffirms that you regret what you did or said.

Ask Forgiveness: "Please forgive me!" This isn't a demand, but a sincere appeal for forgiveness—not to be withdrawn if our mate needs more time or talking.

How hard these steps can be! Especially if you think that you

If a man is alone in

the forest and speaks,

and no woman is around

to hear him....

Is the man still wrong?

UNKNOWN

weren't the only one wrong. It's easy to think, *Why should I be the only one apologizing?*

Why? Because you love your relationship more than being right. In fact, you can be sure that you won't be able to get these words out until you are as ready to forgive as you are to seek forgiveness.

Remember, these steps are intended to help you make a thorough apology, not to use as standards for your husband's apologies. It's been said that the three words a wife loves to hear the most are not "I love you" but "I was wrong"!

One wife confides, "I kept trying to get my husband to apologize to me the right way. I had in mind exactly what I really wanted him to say to assuage my wrath, and he never did. Finally I figured out that he couldn't read my mind. And that I would have to forgive him even if he offered no apology, much less a bad one. It's so hard to do. But now I go to God with it. We talk it out. Sometimes it gets ugly. But eventually He helps me to let it go."

Maybe by now you're thinking, *I'd faint if my husband ever offered me any kind of apology!*

Here's a challenge: Give your husband the very kind of apologies that you long to hear from him. Make them sincere. A well-worded and well-intentioned apology can be miraculous. As James said, "Therefore confess your sins to each other and pray for each other so that you may be healed" (James 5:16).

Dear Lord,
You know the truth: I'm great at receiving a well-
worded apology, but I'm bad at giving one. In fact,
I've not been serious about the art of apologizing
because I'm usually certain that it's me who should
hear one, not give one. Help, Lord! I sense that this is
a huge key for me. If I could learn to ask for
forgiveness well, it would bless my husband greatly.
Let that be my motive. Let me not glory in doing it
but humbly offer whatever apology I owe. Help me to
own what wrong I can, even if I imagine a pile of
wrongs on his side of the fence. In Your powerful,
forgiving name I pray. Amen.

thirty-five

Should We Separate?

*If my aim is love, I don't have to fear
what love may require.*

A PARAPHRASE OF 1 JOHN 4:18

The U-Haul truck parked in our driveway confirmed the reality. Randy was moving away. Not just across town or to a motel for a few nights.

"Deb, how could I allow this to happen?" Randy fought back tears.

The lump that kept rising in my throat gave way to sobs. We held each other and wept. My heart felt as if it had been torn apart. And so began what turned out to be the longest year of our lives.

For the previous twenty years of marriage, I had resisted the idea of separation, insisting that it could not be God's will. But after many years of counseling with professionals, pastors, and attending Al-Anon meetings, I'd come to a place where I believed that Randy needed tough love, and we both needed a break from the tumultuous storm that had become our marriage.

Initially I wasn't strong enough or whole enough as a person to ask Randy for a separation. I had all kinds of excuses: I'll be lonely. I don't want to be responsible for everything: home, finances, caring for our sons. I don't want to feel single. Eventually, however, I became convinced beyond any doubt that I had to do this for Randy—and

200

for me, too, if there was any hope for our marriage to survive.

So after much prayer and counsel with some godly friends, I asked Randy to leave. Among the conditions for us to get back together was the stipulation that Randy had to achieve a substantial period of sobriety (more than the usual couple of weeks he'd succeeded at on occasion). "I love you," I told him. "I love you too much to watch you destroy yourself by drinking. I am committed to you and our marriage forever. I will be here when you are ready to live with me without alcohol."

I bumbled a lot in those first few months, wondering what was best, wondering if there were rules for marital separation. I prayed a lot for wisdom.

Six weeks after Randy moved out, I visited him in his new home. It felt strange seeing half our household settled into unfamiliar surroundings. "Someday this will be our home," Randy promised in a card I found on my pillow. Pain gnawed at my heart. *Will we ever be together again?*

Maybe you, too, have wrestled with the agonizing question of whether a separation might be appropriate for you and your husband. Separation can be an important time-out in a relationship, sometimes for the sake of safety, individual healing, growth, and the ultimate healing of your marriage. However, separation should be a last resort in most cases. It should never be just because we're tired of working on our marriage, are angry, or want to escape.

Some conditions in which separating from your spouse might be best or even crucial include:

- Your husband is caught in a cycle of self-destructive behaviors and refuses to seek help.
- You are on the verge of filing for divorce and are completely out of other options.

- Your husband's behavior is abusive toward you or your children.
- Your husband is participating in something illegal and won't stop.
- Your husband is continuing in an adulterous relationship.
- You and your husband both agree that some distance and a predetermined short time apart to work on the marriage would be a positive thing.

Whatever the reason for separation, check your motives and the wisdom of your plan. Dr. Dan Allender writes in his book *Bold Love*: "Love is a sacrifice for the undeserving that opens the door to restoration of relationship with the Father, with others, and with ourselves."[1]

Ask yourself these questions:

- Am I doing this because I love my husband and want restoration, or am I secretly hoping he'll never come back?
- Am I committed to this course so that I'll be able to sustain it for the long haul?
- Are the conditions for the ending of the separation clear to both of us and specific enough to measure objectively?
- Have I communicated my purposes, my love, and my fidelity to my husband?
- Have I planned the separation carefully when I'm not in a crisis mode, rather than screaming at my husband to get out after we've had a big blow-up?

Before you act, talk with a pastor or counselor to be sure that you know how to talk to your husband about the separation, and to be sure that this is a necessary action to bring about the restoration of your relationship.

Of course, you can do everything right and your husband may not make the changes you long for. That's what makes separation so scary and risky. There are no guarantees. How well I know this!

Randy and I had agreed to separate for a year, and at the end of that time, I felt satisfied that he had made enough progress for us to reunite. We had a happy reunion and all seemed well...for about two months. Then Randy started drinking again.

I pray that I may care enough, to love enough, to share enough to let others become what they can be.

JOHN O'BRIEN

At first I despaired. I was embarrassed and ashamed. How could this happen when I'd felt so sure that separating was the right thing—and that getting back together when we did was equally right? I agonized over whether I should separate again. I prayed and sought wise counsel, and in the end felt that God was leading me to stay with Randy, even though he was drinking again.

In retrospect, I now know that Randy's step backward and my choice to stay with him *didn't* nullify the two steps forward we'd taken together by separating. In many ways, we had had a successful separation. The time apart had confirmed how much we really wanted to live together. It had also taken Randy on a painful but enlightening emotional journey that was part of his eventual recovery.

And I had come to understand that the benefits of separation weren't just about Randy's fulfilling an ultimatum. I, too, had a lot of important inner work I had to do. The separation caused me to lean on God in a way that I never had before. It helped me to be confident that I could live without Randy. And it strengthened my sense of who I was in God's eyes, not just as the wife of an alcoholic.

If you decide you need to separate for a period of time, keep in mind that there are no neat and tidy formulas for the perfect separation. The most important goal is to obey God and to work on the problems that plague your marriage in a way that you couldn't if you were together.

God's definition of a successful marriage—or a successful separation—is one where we are loving boldy, where we, against all odds, are learning how to love as He loves.

In *The Mystery of Marriage,* Mike Mason writes:

> What the Lord expects of a marriage is not always that it be happy and successful. What He wants is not success, but primarily that deep inner quality of faithfulness which, in its capacity to rise above all appearances of failure, is a reflection of the Lord's faithfulness toward a wayward people. That is how we must love one another, with a vowed loved that is not dependent upon happiness nor any of the external hallmarks of success.[2]

> *Dear God,*
> *I need courage, strength, and wisdom to know how to proceed with my marriage. Thank You that love is a gift from You and that even when it must be tough, it cannot fail. Help me to love my husband like You do—unconditionally, yet with a willingness to do what is hard because it's for his best. It is beyond my natural ability. Give me boldness; grow me up, Lord. I'm tired of acting like a child in an adult's body. Help me remember there is no fear in love. Amen.*

thirty-six

Friendly Support

*As iron sharpens iron, so one woman sharpens
another.*

A PARAPHRASE OF PROVERBS 27:17

arm smiles welcomed me as I reluctantly walked into Mary's family room for my first meeting with One Step Further, a Christian support group for women married to alcoholics. Half a dozen women sat on the floor, looking relaxed, laughing and chatting about other topics besides their husbands. We held hands as Mary prayed. "Lord, help us have wisdom and courage, just for today, to change what we can—ourselves. And thanks for bringing Deb tonight." Her calm voice sounded reassuring, even hopeful. I knew instinctively I was in the right place.

Someone offered tea and gently touched my shoulder. "You're not alone, Deb. We've all been where you are. We understand." I pressed a hand to my cheek to catch my tears.

One Step Further became my lifeline—a safe place to talk about my anger, hurt, fear, and frustration over Randy's alcoholism. With this group of empathetic and wise women, I could stop pretending everything was fine and just be myself. I found a level of honesty and trust that I hadn't encountered anywhere else. These women became my closest friends. I could call them in the middle of the night if I needed to talk, and there would always be a willing listener. No one judged me or thought I was a failure as a Christian because I was struggling...*still*. I felt loved and accepted.

We laughed, both together and at ourselves. I began to realize that over the years I had lost my sense of humor. I took most everything way too seriously.

We also found ways to support each other, even when we weren't at a meeting. One woman came up with a code we could use when we talked on the phone: T.A.N.G. stood for "Things Are Not Good." We could use this code when we were with other people and didn't want to say how things were. If one of them called me at home and asked, "How's it going, Deb?" and I said, "Well, it's T.A.N.G. around here tonight," she knew immediately to pray for Randy and me.

One evening a woman's painful story stirred up similar feelings in each of us. We wept together for the entire meeting, grieving the losses of what we had dreamed for our marriages. We felt God's tender touch of healing that night.

This courageous group wasn't afraid to gently offer truth, to point out areas where we kept falling into the same self-defeating behavior patterns. One friend wrote me this bold but loving letter:

> I know how hard it is to struggle out into the bright sunshine after being in the dark for so long. But you can. I've seen glimpses of you and you are truly beautiful. I was thrilled when you made the struggle one day and called me—in tears. I was honored when you dropped the "I'm all right" and said, "I feel I have no self-respect." I was glad to see the REAL DEB getting some air.
>
> I was not so glad when the "other" Deb called back later, facade in place, and apologized for being real. Deb, it

hurts to open yourself up. But you've got to do it someday. You've got to trust someone, and for a brief moment I believe you trusted me. I know this letter may make you angry with me. If that is the case, call me up and tell me. I guess what I'm trying to say, Deb, is that I believe in you, support you, love you. I identify with you. I would appreciate the chance to give away a precious gift I received in much the same manner. So do whatever you want—I'm going to keep believing in you no matter what.

What would we do without friends who help us change what we can and hang in there with us when our lives unravel at the seams?

If you are in a difficult marriage, you need people in your life who can be a place of safety and strength for you. You may find harbor in a one-to-one relationship with a friend, a small group, a Bible study, or any place where you can become honest and vulnerable, where you encourage and support each other to live out biblical truth. When we commit to praying for and carrying each other's burdens, it makes the load lighter and easier to bear.

Don't be afraid to seek out a support group. Your pastor may be able to refer you to a caring counselor or a Christ-centered support group. Other support groups such as Al-Anon can be found in the Yellow Pages (under Alcoholism). Call a counseling center for a directory of the various support groups in your area or check the local newspaper.

At a recent Al-Anon meeting I attended, a hurting newcomer

I often think, how could I have survived without these women?

CLAUDETTE RENNER

approached me afterward. "Thank you for being here," she whispered, on the verge of tears. "I needed to know you existed, that I'm not out there alone." We hugged each other. All I could say was how grateful I felt for the opportunity to offer her the same gift of comfort and support I had received.

> *Dear God,*
> *Thank You for the friends You bring into our lives,*
> *the ones who are closer than even our own family*
> *members. Help me be willing to trust, to share myself*
> *with others, to be open to their ideas and suggestions.*
> *Lord, I want to become a more responsible, more*
> *mature Christian. I'm thankful I don't have to do this*
> *alone. Amen.*

thirty-seven

Smart Ways to Sway Him

*Wives, be respectful and gracious to your husbands,
especially those who don't know My Word and don't
know Me. You can sway your mate toward Me, not
by your words or lengthy sermons, but by what you
do and how you behave. When he sees the purity you
practice in daily decisions, and the devotion you have
toward him and Me, he will be inclined toward Me.
So don't only focus on beauty that is outward, the
kind that has to do with what clothes you wear, how
you apply your makeup, or the size of your waist.
But instead, focus on developing an even more
powerful kind of beauty. This beauty comes from
deep inside and is the result of nurturing a quiet,
gentle spirit and heart set on Me.*

A PARAPHRASE OF 1 PETER 3:1–4

If you are married to a husband who is not a Christian, you
face unique and painful challenges. Maybe you find it hard
not to envy wives who can attend church with their husbands, pray
with them, and experience spiritual intimacy. Sermons on spiritual
unity in marriage only highlight your heart-wrenching dilemma.

That's understandable. And while God doesn't want you to stop longing for what He intended for marriage, He does want you to trust Him with your husband's heart.

Yes, you have a crucial part to play. But too often the way we go about trying to sway our husbands toward God doesn't match up with what God says. Many wives exhaust themselves and their unbelieving husbands with an all-out, but misguided and manipulative, effort to convince their mates to become Christians.

All in good faith, we may invite over Christian friends to "talk" to him. We leave open Bibles all over the house. We turn every conversation to spiritual matters. (When you find yourself looking for the spiritual nuggets in TV commercials, you know you're getting desperate!) While any one of these tactics could have a positive effect, they're more likely to make your husband feel manipulated. And a manipulated man is a resistant one.

But here's good news: You do have power to sway him. *And there's a right way to go about it.*

Most of us have heard sermons on Peter's message for wives found in 1 Peter 3:1–4. Typically these verses are used to teach about submission in marriage. But I believe that Peter is saying something else here that at first you may have missed. He is laying out the formula for how a woman can sway an unbelieving man's heart toward God.

The Scripture reads:

> Wives, in the same way be submissive to your husbands so that, if any of them do not believe the word, they may be won over without words by the behavior of their wives, when they see the purity and reverence of your lives. Your beauty should not come from outward adornment, such as braided hair and the wearing of gold jewelry and fine

clothes. Instead, it should be that of your inner self, the unfading beauty of a gentle and quiet spirit, which is of great worth in God's sight. (1 Peter 3:1–4)

Peter's words offer four guidelines:

Do it without words. Peter obviously understood that a wife's first inclination is to preach to her husband or try to verbally convince him to receive Christ. But as a man and a husband, he also knew that nagging, badgering, and lecturing would get them nowhere. If anything, their sermons and pleadings would backfire. Instead, Peter urged wives to speak with their lives instead of their mouths.

God, without your help, can get through to your husband much more effectively than you can. In fact, if your voice is too loud in your husband's ear, it may even keep him from hearing God's still, quiet voice.

Katrina remembers well when she first discovered how she needed to stop talking and let the Holy Spirit work in her husband's heart. She says, "John, who is unsaved, always resisted going to church with me, even on holidays like Easter. After wheedling and outright begging for several years, I finally gave up on the idea and kept going alone. Then one Sunday, out of the blue, John wanted to go. I was so surprised. I figured that he'd finally come to see the good reasons behind my arguments in favor of church attendance all those years. Later, when I gently asked why he had the change of heart, he said he realized that a lot of his resistance had been because he was so busy resisting me. 'When you gave it up,' he explained, 'I finally felt free to go.'"

This doesn't mean a woman can't be forthcoming about the part God is playing in her life or how He touched her at work today. The goal isn't that our husbands never hear a peep out of our

mouths about God, but that we refrain from sermonizing, spiritu-
alizing, and otherwise pressuring them with the gospel or with our
spiritual insights.

Do it by your behavior. The second guideline Peter gives is that
we say something to our husbands *through our actions*. Ask yourself:
What can I do today to show my husband Christ's mercy? What
might I do today to communicate love and generosity? How can my
actions today speak loudly some of those words I'm always so
tempted to speak?

These acts might be simple things such as:

- Taking the car through the car wash.
- Rubbing his shoulders for ten minutes after he comes home.
- Cleaning up his bathroom counter for him.

Or they might mean something more sacrificial. You decide to
forgo the new couch you want so that he can buy a new power saw.

How do you prioritize and spend your time and energy? If your
husband was watching closely, would your daily routines demonstrate God's importance in your life? Would they demonstrate that
the message of the gospel is redemptive and joyous? Does your life
in general make the gospel appealing? Or does your behavior communicate that being a Christian is mainly a drudgery and a list of
don'ts to obey?

Do it by exhibiting purity and reverence. Peter encourages
women to woo their husbands to Christ through demonstrating
purity and reverence in their character—not as they imagine or
might describe it, but as their husbands "see" it ("when they see the
purity and reverence…").

Do "purity and reverence" describe you in action? Is there an area of your life—in what you watch, read, or listen to—that is muddying the waters of your spirit?

Remember, all of Peter's advice in this passage comes under the general heading of submission, and reverence is closely related. Synonyms include *admiration* and *respect*. Some examples of showing reverence or respect are not contradicting him in public, asking his opinion on important household matters, listening to him without interrupting, and thanking and appreciating him.

Do it by developing inner beauty. Peter's saying, "Okay, ladies. You know men. They're pretty wrapped up in the physical beauty of a woman. They like a nice physical form and lovely features. But guess what? The thing that will really sway them toward God has nothing to do with what you look like on the outside. The only kind of beauty that will reach into their hearts and direct them toward God is inward beauty. Beauty of spirit, beauty of personality, beauty of character."

What kind of changes would you make if you were to take this to heart? What would happen if you spent more time every day on your spiritual, inner beauty than on your outward beauty? (We're not telling you to neglect your beauty regimen or go back to wearing ratty underwear! A beautiful woman inside and out is the idea).

If you have a gentle, quiet spirit it means you are not pushy, bossy, self-seeking. Remember, gentle doesn't mean weak; it can be defined as "strength under control." And quiet is a reference to a spirit of serenity and peacefulness, not the volume of your voice.

As you set out to win over your husband for Christ, always keep in mind this truth: You're not the only person God can and will use to influence your husband. His means are unlimited. And unlike you, He is in the business of changing lives.

Dear Lord,
How easily I get confused! How easily I go from
swaying to manipulating. Sometimes I can't even sort
out the difference! Give me wisdom to know when
I'm not using my power but taking advantage of it.
Give me wisdom to know when to be quiet and how
to show my husband more than I can say. Cleanse
me of those sins and habits that don't glorify You,
that wouldn't attract anyone, much less my husband!
Thank You, above all, that even though I can't
change my husband—you can! Lord, help me to rest
in that. Amen.

VOICES: TWYLA'S STORY

When Twyla married Gary, she felt certain that eventually he'd accept the Lord. But Gary had other plans, and they didn't include Christ. Soon, Twyla found herself in a very difficult marriage, one which challenged many of her ideas about what it means to be a Christian and a wife.

Even though I knew better, I married an unbeliever. I just knew Gary would give in and accept Christ. After all, my mother-in-law was a saint and she'd been praying that her son would marry a Christian. I figured that I was an answer to her prayer! I convinced myself that our marriage would be an exception to God's prohibition about being unequally yoked in marriage.

Was I ever wrong!

Not only was Gary completely opposed to Christianity, he was a controller. Almost everything had to be his way, regardless of what anyone else thought or felt. He tried to control me, and then our son. We hardly had any choices, even if he pretended we did. He would ask us what restaurant we'd like to go to for dinner, but then he'd criticize every place we named until we landed on the one that he wanted to go to all along. Eventually we figured out how to know which restaurant "we" were all hungry for that night: Just ask Gary!

Twyla's Story

Over the years I stopped expressing my opinion, because if I did and it was contrary to Gary's thinking, then my life was full of turmoil, strife, and tension. I decided I would do everything in my power to get along with Gary and not fight with him. I've always despised arguing because it seems arrogant. Arguing says, "I'm right and you're wrong. My way is better than yours." I calmly stated my beliefs and feelings, but Gary never seemed to listen. But I knew God knew my heart, my motives.

I decided that Gary was God's problem; the battle in our marriage was God's to fight, not mine. I tried to take to heart the Bible's command to live with men at peace as much as possible. It wasn't always easy. But when I succeeded, life was much more pleasant for both of us.

I made plenty of mistakes along the way. I didn't always know, as a Christian, how I should respond in difficult situations, like the time when Gary invited our son's girlfriend to move in with us. Gary had visited her tiny, run-down apartment and insisted she come to our house to live—indefinitely. Our son was only a senior in high school, while his girlfriend was a year older. Gary hadn't consulted me, and I felt hurt and angry. I cried for days on end. He never knew how close I came to leaving him at that point.

One day I came across those passages of Scripture that tell us to bless our enemies, and if someone slaps you on one side of the cheek, to offer him the other. If someone asks you to go one mile, go with him two. I kept thinking about all these verses. They seemed doable if I imagined carrying them out with some stranger. But when I thought of them in terms of my husband, they seemed impossible!

Nevertheless, I begged God to help me do my best to bless my husband rather than to retaliate every time he hurt me. I accepted the arrangement of having our son and his girlfriend under the same roof. They each had separate bedrooms, but it was still awkward and trying. I stuck it out and made the best of the situation.

My son and his girlfriend did get married, and today she tells me how much my loving response meant to her. "Only godly love truly knows how to love unselfishly," she says.

Sometimes other women accused me of being a doormat. "You have rights, Twyla," they'd tell me. I would tell them that I knew I had rights, but that I was choosing to give up those rights. I was putting them into God's safekeeping. Over the years I learned that letting go was the path to a place of true freedom. I was no longer a slave to my husband's anger and rejection. I didn't need his approval and affirmation, but sought them instead from God.

For example, when Gary went into a verbal tirade, I'd think of his angry words as a coat. If he belittled me or didn't like what I'd fixed for dinner or how I'd arranged the furniture, I refused to put on the coat. I refused to dwell on his verbal abuse or to allow his criticism to snatch my joy. I chose not to take his insults personally. I'd calmly listen to him, acknowledge his feelings, then go about my business. My refusal to retaliate usually diffused any hostility on Gary's part. Our marriage didn't change a lot, but my attitudes did, and I grew more Christlike in my response to him.

A few years ago, Gary was diagnosed with terminal cancer. Six months before his death, he made a commitment to Christ. Our twenty-six years of marriage ended with forgiveness and reconciliation. Now that he's gone, my suffering seems insignificant. In the end apart from Christ, I was never any better than Gary, anyway! Just forgiven.

I have no regrets about staying married to Gary. The marriage never got easier, but I gained in ways that matter: inner peace and a close relationship with God.

thirty-eight

One Day at a Time

For this reason, my dear sisters, be constant,
unyielding, always giving yourselves fully to the
Lord's work, which includes your marriage. You can
be sure that everything you do for the Lord is never
wasted effort.

A PARAPHRASE OF 1 CORINTHIANS 15:58

t was another gray, drizzly November day, the week before
Thanksgiving. Why do crises come right before the holidays?
Randy's drinking was out of control again—after several treatment
programs, counseling, and trial separations. One more drink
seemed to be all that mattered to him, but with Christmas only a
month away, I wanted to pretend that everything was okay.

But I couldn't. I'd come too far to hide my head in the sand.

How I wrestled and raged at God that morning. Why hadn't He
answered my prayers about Randy? Did I lack faith? Was I foolish
to stay in this marriage when Randy continued to drink? Should I
just give up—after twenty years—and walk away? Was that what
God wanted me to do?

My grief overwhelmed me. I was at a loss. For years I'd clung
to the belief that if Randy only accepted Christ, he would be healed
of his alcoholism and our problems would be solved.

That morning I admitted I'd been wrong.

Just a few months before, Randy had gone forward in church and prayed to receive Christ. His decision stunned me. When we were first married, Randy had shown no interest in Christianity, and I became obsessed with trying to convert him. Of course it didn't work, and eventually I gave up hope, even when he started coming to church. But God worked in Randy's heart despite my wavering faith. God's will was accomplished, in His perfect timing.

I was thrilled, of course, and truly believed Randy's drinking days were gone at last. And Randy did stop drinking—for a week or two. He tried to change; he prayed for change—but still he craved a drink. He was depressed and frustrated, disappointed in himself and God.

And so was I.

A few weeks later, the week before Christmas, Randy once again went forward in church for prayer and confessed his continuing struggle with alcoholism. Our pastor, Mark, responded, "We will never give up on you, Randy, and neither will the Lord." He rested his head on Randy's, like a father. "I love you so much, but not even close to how much God loves you. The Father's arms are wide open. He wants to welcome you home. It doesn't matter what you've done, where you've been, how far you've gotten off the path."

Randy wept openly. So did Mark and the rest of us. "As a church family, we will stand beside you forever. We will never stop praying for you and believing that God will heal you. He won't allow you to lose this battle. Oh, Lord, please help our beloved friend."

Once again I hoped, and once again Randy's drinking got worse instead of better. What was God doing?

On Christmas Eve, Randy sat in front of the TV drunk. He had

Do you suppose your Father will let you carry the banner of His victory and His gladness on to the front of the battle, and then coolly stand back and see you captured or beaten back by the enemy? Never! The Holy Spirit will sustain you in your bold advances, and fill your heart with gladness and praise, and you will find your heart all exhilarated and refreshed by the fullness within.

STREAMS IN THE DESERT

stopped at a bar on his way home from last minute shopping. He fell asleep on the couch and didn't wake up until the next morning, missing our usual family holiday traditions. I felt so angry and betrayed that I left the house and stayed with my friend Judy that night. It was the most lonely, depressing Christmas I'd ever experienced. How could I continue to watch Randy destroy himself? Why continue to hope?

Have you ever reached bottom like this? Have you ever wondered if you are crazy to stay when it seems like there is no hope of change?

At such times we want to give up in defeat.

And at such times we need perseverance.

When we think about perseverance, we think of exertion. We imagine a runner sprinting to the finish line, chin jutted forward, legs straining, face dripping with sweat. But we have it wrong. Perseverance isn't about working harder; it's about *not quitting in the face of opposition.*

And that's what perseverance often looks like for a wife in a not-so-perfect marriage. We resolve to keep trying. We don't quit. We stand firm in our commitment; we insist on staying when we want to run.

We persevere, one day at a time.

Singer Margaret Becker writes this about perseverance, "When we have the courage to meet obstacles head on and the tenacity to hang on through discouraging detours, grace is our reward. We emerge from the battle more Christlike than at the beginning."[1]

Six years ago, Randy and I moved away from our home church. But we visited there again recently. Pastor Mark, who is now pastor at a different church, had returned to preach that Sunday. Once again we felt surrounded by the love of a congregation who understands the meaning of perseverance. These dear people still haven't given up on Randy and on our marriage. They continue to pray; they continue to hope.

I think our reunion at Wabash Church was only a preview of the grand reunion waiting for us someday in heaven, where every tear and memory of those discouraging detours will be washed away.

So don't give up. Keep going. One day at a time.

> *Dear God,*
> *I admit there are times when I want to give up. My*
> *faith is weak, and I doubt anything good can ever*
> *come from our circumstances. Help me learn the*
> *lessons of perseverance, of loving my husband and*
> *desiring to hold up a godly standard for our*
> *marriage. Lord, I humbly give thanks for all who*
> *have persevered in loving us. Without them, I would*
> *have quit the race a long time ago. Because of Your*
> *faithfulness to us, I press on toward the finish. All*
> *praise to You! Amen.*

thirty-nine

Promise Centered

*Finally, my sisters in Christ, if you focus on what is
true and good and right, and dwell on what is good
in your husband instead of being critical, you can't
help but have a more positive outlook.*

A PARAPHRASE OF PHILIPPIANS 4:8

halfway house in Oregon has an expectation of its residents. All communication between individuals or in small groups needs to be promise centered instead of problem centered. When anyone starts whining or complaining, the others are supposed to offer the reminder: "Promise centered, not problem centered." That way they focus on hope. Change, transformation, and healing are possible, rather than getting bogged down in the quagmire of despair and hopelessness. We would do well to adapt this approach to communication with our husbands, reminding ourselves often to focus on the promise, not the problem.

Here are some ways we can use promise-centered communication:

- Try encouraging instead of complaining, nagging, or being critical. Let your husband know you appreciate him. Thank him when he does something helpful, such as unloading the dishwasher or picking up groceries on his way home from work.

Simple courtesies go a long way in building a more amicable relationship. Focus on what's right, not what's wrong.

- Develop positive ways to discuss problems. Be honest but loving in expressing your feelings. Use *I* statements, such as, "*I* feel disappointed when you forget my birthday," rather than, "*You* always forget my birthday."
- Don't threaten your husband with getting a divorce or other ultimatums unless you've thoroughly considered the outcome. Try to reason things out, looking at possible solutions, not impossible problems.
- Be sensitive when you talk with others about your husband. Be careful not to gossip or slander him.

Being in a promise-centered marriage means you rely on God's promises to carry you through the tough times. The Bible is filled with encouragement; it is God's assurance that He will bring good from even the most difficult situations, that no one is beyond His reach for redemption, that He will never leave us or forsake us. And those only represent a few of the numerous ways He promises to care for us. God's Word offers the ultimate model for promise-centered living. For example, 1 Corinthians 13 defines love: "It always protects, always trusts, always hopes, always perseveres. Love never fails" (vv. 7–8). We just have to believe! That may be the most difficult aspect of faith, believing God's promises are real. They are there for us to plug into our lives.

"Nothing will ever be different in my marriage," Janet used to complain to her friends. "George doesn't know how to communicate, to tell me how he feels, what he's thinking about. I can't remember when he last told me he loved me. I might as well be single."

Janet's friends assured her that even though her marriage looked bleak on the outside, she still had the promise of becoming

> Since we cannot change reality, let us change the eyes which see reality.
>
> NIKOS KAZANTZAKIS

a new creation in Christ within her marriage. As she grew in her relationship with the Lord, she was certain to change. It's guaranteed, one of God's promises! Because of her growth, her marriage had hope for taking on new, refreshing characteristics, even if Janet was the only person who changed.

To Janet's surprise, time proved her wise friends correct. She stopped complaining about everything that she thought was wrong with her marriage. She even began to notice and appreciate her husband's good qualities, ways he said *I love you* without words. He got up early to put the coffee on, made sure her car was warmed up and defrosted on winter mornings, and called her at work each day just to say hi. Today, Janet doesn't focus on the problems. Instead, she sees the promise of transformation in her marriage. If God could change her, wasn't it also possible for her husband to change?

Perspective is everything. It's easy to be drawn to wallowing in negatives, not seeing glimmers of hope, discounting gains and changes which have occurred. As long as we focus on what's wrong, we may be standing in the way of what the Lord can do in and through us.

I like the halfway house's method of operation: "Promise centered." My heart feels lighter just saying those words.

Dear Lord,

It's much easier to complain about what's wrong than to see what's right in my marriage. Help me focus on the promise of change and growth, if only in myself. Thank You for Your Word that gives me a pattern for living. I would be lost without it and overwhelmed by our problems. With Your help, Lord, I will look for the promise of hope in our marriage. Amen.

forty

When It Hurts
to Hope

But as for me, I will always have hope; I will praise
you more and more. Why should I allow myself to feel
downcast? I choose to put my hope and my marriage
in God's hands, knowing that I will yet praise him, my
Savior and my God.

A PARAPHRASE OF PSALM 71:14; 42:11

How much hope do you have that someday your marriage will be all you ever dreamed of? How much hope do you have for change in yourself? In your husband?

Should you have hope?

Let's face it. Sometimes it hurts to hope. It's easier to give up believing for a change in our marriages, to give up on the possibility that something good is around the corner. After all, we've held out hope so many times only to end up disappointed.

Corrina and Peter have been married for twelve years. For almost as long, Corrina has been clinging to the hope that her husband will agree to go to counseling with her and get help with his anger problem. Today, Peter seems no nearer to acquiescing than he did ten years ago. "I've quit believing that Peter will ever change or even want to. It only hurts to keep hoping," says Corrina. "It's sad.

But I finally decided that the pain of hoping and getting disappointed was worse than the pain of abandoning all hope. I guess it's a way to protect myself."

Chances are that your friends have said to you about your husband or your marriage, "Just don't give up hope." What do they mean? And why do we say this to one another when things look bad? What are we afraid will happen if the person gives up hope?

We fear despair. And we sense that if a person gives up hoping, the desired end will be even less likely to happen. We might as well dig a grave.

Maybe this is because when hope is abandoned, so is faith. Hope is different than faith, but it's closely connected. If I have some hope that my marriage will improve, then I believe improvement is possible. But if I have faith that it will—I've taken it to the next step: *I not only believe it is a possibility, I believe it will happen, and I act as though it will.* If we give up hope, then faith becomes impossible.

We know God commands us to have faith, and since we can't have faith without hope, he wants us to have hope as well. In Romans 12:12, Paul writes, "Be joyful in hope, patient in affliction, faithful in prayer."

Repeatedly, the Bible admonishes us to hold on to hope. But the problem comes when we hold on to the result we hope for, rather than hope itself.

In *The Marriage Builder,* Larry Crabb writes:

> The hope of the Christian is not that one's spouse will change or that one's health will improve or that one's financial situation will become good…. Our responsibility is to respond to life's events in a manner intended to please the Lord, not to change our spouse into what we want. And if we do respond biblically, we have no guarantee that our

Hope is hearing the
melody of the future.
Faith is the dance to it.

UNKNOWN

spouses will respond in kind. Though they file for divorce or continue to drink or nag all the more, yet there is reason for us to persevere.... Our spouses may not do what they should to restore our marriage to happy, fulfilling relationships. But if we remain faithful to God, pouring our emotions before Him, renewing our commitment to seek him, trusting Him to guide us in our responses, then He will sustain us in our trials.... There is reason to go on. There is hope."[1]

We can hope for our husbands to change. We can hope for our marriages to improve. But *ultimately,* we must hope for more. Our hope is that in all things, God will be at work. Our hope is that He will be changing us daily, rescuing us from false hopes, from hopes that have to do only with what we can see right now, hopes that are too small, hopes that have little to do with eternity.

Ultimately, *He* is our hope. Our hope is not in what time might accomplish. Our hope is not in what we can do to get our husbands to see the light. If our hope is in *Him,* if our hope is in His will being carried out in our marriages in His time, it is *impossible* that our hope will be disappointed.

Dear Lord,
How grateful I am that You do not give up hope on
me even when I lose sight of the good You want to
accomplish in my marriage. Help me to never give
up hope on You or on what You can do in my
marriage. You always give me reason to hope. You
never give me reason to despair. Today I will put my
faith in You alone. Amen.

forty-one

Amazing Grace

*I waited patiently for the Lord to restore my
marriage; He turned to me and heard my cry. He
lifted my husband and me up from the sludge of our
misery and set us on a solid foundation where we
could stand. He has given us a new song, and we will
sing a hymn of praise to our God.*

A PARAPHRASE OF PSALM 40:1–3

Three years ago I had closed my heart to Randy after yet
another relapse, determined not to be hurt anymore. I had
even asked for another separation, and Randy had moved in
with a friend.

But God had another plan. A new interim pastor and his wife
approached me after their first Sunday with our congregation. "I
really think we can help you, Deb, if you and Randy are willing. It
would be a privilege to counsel with you."

"I don't know," I replied. "We've already been through lots of
programs, counseling, treatment centers. Nothing has made a difference."

Neil and Ruth didn't have any preconceived ideas of success.
They simply offered to meet with us after the worship service each
week. Randy and I reluctantly agreed to give counseling another

chance. We spent every Sunday afternoon together that summer. We shared picnic lunches, hiked, talked, poured out our anger and pain, and listened to Neil and Ruth's godly wisdom. We had homework. "What is it about each other that you truly appreciate?" Neil asked. "Write it down and bring your lists next week."

Neil asked us to memorize Scriptures such as Philippians 4: 8–9: "Finally, brothers, whatever is true, whatever is noble, whatever is right, whatever is pure, whatever is lovely, whatever is admirable—if anything is excellent or praiseworthy—think about such things." We paraphrased Psalm 1 and talked about the armor of God, how each piece could help us fight the battle to restore our marriage.

We remembered the good times, wept over the heartbreaking experiences of our marriage, and grieved all we had lost. We yelled, told the truth about how we felt, and forgave each other for our sins.

During this time, Randy stopped drinking. Yet, it felt as though we were finally focused on working on our marriage, not just on Randy's sobriety.

By the end of summer, we talked about "getting married" again. Randy seemed to have made a lasting breakthrough to sobriety. But understandably, I was skeptical and frightened. After four treatment programs and twenty-seven years of marriage, could the miracle I'd been praying for finally have taken place?

As I considered whether the miracle of Randy's sobriety would last, it dawned on me that maybe the *real* miracle had come long ago, in ways I hadn't expected. It had slowly but unmistakably happened in me: in changed attitudes, in the ability to love someone who wasn't easy to love, in offering forgiveness even when I didn't feel like it, in believing without a doubt that nothing—even marriage to an alcoholic—is impossible with God.

> Celebration can really come about only where fear and love, joy and sorrow, tears and smiles can exist together.
>
> HENRI NOUWEN

And so it was that I said "I do" to Randy once again.

Neil told us that by getting married again, we would be saying to God, ourselves, and the rest of the world that we were starting over, building a new marriage. The old one had defects and needed to be torn down and rebuilt with new materials. "What are you willing to bring to the new structure to make it strong and long lasting?" he asked. Randy promised godly sorrow for his actions, patience, understanding of my concerns, tenderness and compassion, and humility. I offered forgiveness, love, hope, honesty, and the willingness to become vulnerable, risking the possibility of being hurt again.

On a golden morning that same fall, our loved ones packed the little log church. Friends from our old Seattle neighborhood and my support group drove over for the occasion. They insisted that the bride shouldn't spend the night before the wedding with the groom, so we girls enjoyed the evening together. We laughed, cried, and celebrated what God had done in all our lives, especially the miracle of a new fresh start for Randy and me. Again.

We stood before the congregation on our second wedding day with our sons, Chris and Jeremy, as our best men. We took our vows more seriously, with much more insight and understanding than we had at nineteen. And we promised to uphold them. God had faithfully brought us through the rough times. He would see us through this new beginning in our lives. The blue icing on our wedding cake spelled out our story: Amazing Grace. And it is.

I waited a long time, twenty-seven years, for Randy to stop drinking. Today, almost four years later, I rejoice in Randy's continued sobriety. But even more, I rejoice that we are still married. And I take it one day at a time.

Looking back, I see that I've made a lot of mistakes. I haven't always chosen the wisest path for myself, Randy, and our sons. Sometimes I'd like to rewind and do over big sections of my life. But then I realize that without all those mistakes and stops and starts, we wouldn't be here. I see now that many times when I had imagined we were going backward, we really were falling forward. Toward God, toward each other, toward love.

You, too, may wonder at times if you're making any progress at all. Maybe like me you are waiting for a miracle to take place in your husband, while all along it's happening in you. Can you see it? During all the days, weeks, and years when your marriage felt painful and love seemed impossible, a beautiful, mysterious miracle has been taking shape. And with every tear you cry, every sin you forgive, and every exhausted prayer you pray, it still is.

This is why you can say with confidence, "I know my Redeemer lives," even if you're sitting in an ash heap like Job. You don't know what the future holds for your marriage, but you do know Who holds the future. You don't know how, when, or if your marriage will become all you dream. But because you said forever, you have decided to stay and keep falling forward into love.

This is the miracle of marriage, and this is my prayer for you:

May the God of all grace, who gives endurance, encouragement, and hope to every wife who asks, accomplish His purposes in you and in your marriage. May you always remember that He can and will do more than you can even ask or imagine because of His exceedingly great power and love for you. And may this power, which was strong enough to raise Jesus from the dead, be at work in you and in the husband you love until death do you part. Amen. (Romans 15:5, 13; Ephesians 3:20; 1 Peter 1:21)

The publisher and author would love to hear your comments about this book. *Please contact us at:* www.multnomah.net/forever

Appendix

HARD QUESTIONS

1. What should I do if my husband hurts me physically?
If you've been mistreated by the one who promised to cherish you, first, a small note of solace: You aren't alone, and neither is the abuse about *you*. Unfortunately, physical abuse is as prevalent in marriages where husband and wife are professing Christians as in marriages between nonbelievers. Some studies show that such abuse is more common in "religious fundamentalist" homes. In the U.S., this points to Christian homes, a disturbing reality. A reality so baffling, in fact, it's often ignored by church leaders, compounding the pain of an injured wife.

God's pattern for husbands is to love their wives as Christ loved the church (Ephesians 5:25). Love doesn't hurt. When God asks that wives be submissive, it is to the anticipated love and nurture of a godly man. His will for you doesn't include physical harm, even when couched in "playful" jostling or "scriptural" justification. Nothing you could ever do warrants mistreatment.

Experts, both in and outside the church, agree: *Physical abuse is not an option in any marriage.* If your husband shoves or slaps you, don't ignore it. If he hurts you, it is technically abuse and can be dangerous. You may not be able to help your husband with that problem in the short term, but if you take a stand the first time he hurts you, the better your chances of reconciling with your husband on a long-term basis.

If your husband hits, shoves, kicks, slaps, beats, throws, or harms you in any way that causes bruises, abrasions, welts, or broken bones:

- Remove yourself and your children immediately and go to a place where you will be safe—to the home of a relative or friend or to a community shelter.
- Do not communicate with your husband until you are safe and only in the presence of a third party who supports you.
- Get in touch with a counselor; if necessary, seek one through a church or a nonprofit private or public agency that assists families. Find someone who will listen to you and speak in your behalf. The National Domestic Violence Hotline can be contacted at (800) 799-SAFE or TDD (800) 787-3224
- Don't return to your husband and put your life or your children's lives at risk simply because he seems genuinely remorseful and promises not to hurt you again. The fact is, he most likely will. Experts have documented the abuse cycle. With few exceptions, their research has shown that if a man hasn't put himself in counseling or a recovery program, his anger will flare again, sometimes followed by progressively greater force. Again, this will be followed by sincere repentance, a calm period, repetitive abuse, and so on.
- Seek support and guidance. If appropriate, initiate reconciliation based on your husband's willingness to change his behavior. Under all circumstances, involve a third party in this process.

In the meantime, God offers this promise to you: "For your Maker is your husband—the LORD Almighty is His name—the

Holy One of Israel is your Redeemer" (Isaiah 54:5). In the days ahead, read the entire chapter of Isaiah 54 as you accept the protection and comfort of the Lord.

2. What should I do if my husband is addicted to alcohol or drugs, and he won't get help?

If your spouse is refusing to get help, he's denying that he has a problem. Often, the worse the addiction, the deeper the denial. The deeper the denial, the more creative the coping mechanisms and the longer before reaching a state of desperation. Again, you can't force your husband to get help if he doesn't want it.

But there are some things you can do:

Admit that you are living with an addicted person. This first step often requires incredible courage and fortitude, but until those people closest to an addicted person stop denying the extent of the problem, the abuser is that much more sheltered from it, as well.

Talk to a counselor or find a support group such as Al-Anon. You'll need emotional support and professional guidance on how to respond to specific behaviors.

Enlist a prayer partner who will pray for you daily—with vigor—because you're going to need it. Ask that person to pray a hedge of protection around you, and a veil of wisdom over you.

An addict is often an expert at keeping telltale signs well hidden; after all, he has already created an amazing network of lies in his own mind. Lies to his wife are only an extension of that. This kind of subterfuge is one reason why addictions carry a legacy of spiritual and emotional oppression that affects everybody in the home. You may not even notice because oppression starts to feel normal. You and your family need prayer, regular worship with a community of faith, and engagement with the disciplines of the Christian life.

Make it your business to know more about your husband's addiction than he does. As you work at deciding what is healthy and wise, you'll continually realign your choices regarding your relationship with your husband. Talk to as many experts as you can and read a wide variety of material, including professional works on individual addictions.

Determine what your boundaries will be. At what point should you draw the line—when the addiction threatens your children physically? emotionally? How many relapses should you allow for? Will you allow illegal substances in the house? Is your husband selling drugs as well as using them? How often? Are you supposed to watch him go through the consequences of addiction: losing his job, alienating friends, or going to prison? You'll want to talk these questions over with a counselor, but ultimately the boundaries are up to you.

Take care of yourself. Make sure you are getting enough rest and nutrition and exercise so that you don't get run down. If you are *not* getting what you need, you won't be able to help your children or your spouse deal with the irregular circumstances of your lives.

3. At what point do my husband's verbal barbs become emotional abuse? On the surface, the answer to this question is simple. Whenever words hurt your feelings, they abuse. Verbal remarks by your husband are experienced by you as emotional abuse when you are:

- The object of cruel jokes
- Insulted, called names
- Ordered about
- Taunted
- Dominated

- Screamed at
- Falsely blamed
- Unfairly accused
- Invalidated
- Discounted
- The object of cursing
- Undermined
- Trivialized
- Unfairly criticized
- Threatened

In many instances, it's not the words or the attack itself that is so wounding as the way we process it. According to the National Clearinghouse on Family Violence, "Emotional abuse can have serious physical and psychological consequences for women, including severe depression, anxiety, persistent headaches, back and limb problems, and stomach problems. Women who are psychologically abused but not physically abused are five times more likely to misuse alcohol than women who have not experienced abuse."[1]

You can't change your husband, but you *can* change your response to his verbal abuse. Here are some guidelines:

- Refuse to engage in conversations that involve verbal abuse. When your husband threatens you or otherwise crosses any of the lines in the list above, tell him calmly that you won't be able to continue the discussion. First, however, give him fair warning. List for him ahead of time those specific behaviors that cause you the most pain and explain that from now on you will have to end any discussion in which they are a part.
- Tell him how deeply his words wound you. Many husbands don't realize just how much damage they do with unkind

words. Choose a time when you are getting along well to tell your husband, "Honey, did you know that when you say _____, I feel _____? Is that what you intend?" Ask him if he, too, would like to talk to you about what you say or how you behave when you're angry. Make it a mutual problem, not just his.

- Battle lies with truth. Make a list of the things your husband says about you and ask God if there is any legitimacy to the charges there and, if so, to help you change. Then spend time focusing on the truth, God's truth—about who you are, what you are, what you do.

- Defuse explosive situations. If your husband is angry, yelling, and blowing his stack, this isn't the time to battle back, and it may not even be the time to walk away. Listen calmly and say things like "I hear what you're saying" and "Can you please not yell?" until he calms down. However, if you sense that he is about to become violent, remove yourself immediately to a safe place, even if it means locking a door against your husband.

- Don't reward verbal abuse. If your spouse finds he can intimidate or control you with verbal barbs, they're likely to fly. But if you refuse to be coerced, swayed, or convinced by arguments he makes in verbally abusive ways, he'll have to look for other, perhaps more direct, ways to speak to you.

- Ask your husband to seek help and consider it yourself, as well. Anyone who is chronically abusive is usually feeling disempowered himself—on the job, with a parent or sibling, in a period of depression, or wrestling with some temptation. His need is to validate himself, and he may accomplish that by invalidating you. If he has a chronic or escalating problem, choose a good time to talk to him about getting professional help or attending an anger management group. If he is resistant, at least be sure he knows about his options should he change his mind. In the meantime, you should consider seeking counsel to help you cope with his behavior.

4. What if my husband refuses to be responsible to work and support our family?
Believe it or not, the pathos behind this question is not uncommon. If your husband is not working and bringing in income, what can you do?

Determine whether there's a legitimate employment problem involved. There might be reasons your husband refuses to work that are related to his occupation or work history. Has he suffered from chronic job loss? He could lack crucial skills for employment. Did he initiate a frequent change of employers? It could be that he's not cut out to work for anyone other than himself. Sometimes men can't find work in their area of education or expertise, and this is hard. If this is the case, try to problem solve. Is there a job he could do from home? Does he have a hobby that could be turned into an income? Maybe college, technical school, or a community college retraining program is appropriate.

Examine your role. When a husband isn't working, most wives will simply pick up the responsibility, go to work or get more work, and carry on. What they may not realize is that one husband may feel intimidated by a wife's ability to get things done, while another man may think, *Look what I've got here; I'll just let her do it.* The wife is doing so much that there's nothing left for him to do—and he likes it that way. Sometimes the woman does too. After all, the one who controls the purse strings often has the power.

Are you doing too much—and allowing your husband to act simply as a consumer rather than as a contributor to the marriage? If so, decide just how much you should work. You want to support your family financially, but without buffering him from hard realities and his own responsibilities.

Find ways to boost his self-esteem. Don't berate your husband. Chances are he's already suffering from low self-esteem. One key to getting him back to work is to help him feel good enough about himself that he has the emotional energy to pursue employment. Try to get him busy with activities he enjoys and is good at. Encourage him to be physically active, which is a natural feel-good boost. Point out as many positive things about him as you can, whenever you can. Finally, be sure not to rule out serious depression or chemical imbalances. Maybe it's time for a checkup.

Offer your husband the opportunity to act responsibly. If he isn't working, see if he would be willing to take over household chores, such as grocery shopping, cleaning, laundry, ironing, cooking dinner, and preparing the kids' lunches. This not only lessens your load, but it also enables him to keep his self-respect because he is carrying part of the load.

Redeem the days. As hard as it might be, find ways to maximize this opportunity for your marriage. Look for the benefits that come from having a lot of time together and ask yourself what good can come out of this season in your lives. One wife whose husband was unemployed for two years says, "Now I wonder, why, instead of nagging all day and fighting with him, didn't I take advantage of having him around? Now that he's back to working full time with a lot of overtime, I realize I missed some opportunities."

5. How can I know if my husband is molesting my kids, and if he is, what should I do about it?
First, whether you suspect abuse or not, take steps to prevent it. In *Real Solutions for Abuse-Proofing Your Child*, Dr. Grace Ketterman, a Christian child psychiatrist and pediatrician, advises all parents to:

Be sure your child knows that it is NEVER acceptable for ANYONE to touch his or her private parts, and that if someone does, to tell you about it immediately.

Tell your child that he or she can talk to you about *anything*. Be sure you respond to whatever they tell you with wisdom, grace and acceptance. Don't judge or react negatively.

Educate yourself and your child. Certain school programs teach kids how to recognize sexual abuse and discern inappropriate touch from what's appropriate. Inquire at your local school district, look up information in the library or on the Internet. There are lots of golden moments at home to share the basic facts about sex abuse while using age-friendly language. A few simple slogans go a long way toward helping kids have the courage to say no, move away from an offender, and "tell, tell, tell." Knowing there is a name to unwarranted touching dilutes fear and gives kids freedom to express their own feelings about it. It will prevent them from being conned into believing molestation is normal or should be tolerated from an authority figure.[2]

If you suspect, even faintly, that your husband may be molesting one or more of your children, don't ignore your feelings! Trust your instincts and do your best to uncover the truth. This is the most loving thing you can do for both your child and your husband. Your responsibility is to protect your child, not your husband. The earlier you step in, the less damage to the mental health of your child and the greater the chance of healing for your spouse.

If you find yourself in this situation, take these steps:

Pray for discernment.

Pay close attention to how your spouse relates to the child. Dr. Ketterman advises that if all of a sudden one of your children can do no wrong in the eyes of your husband or gets special privileges, you should begin to explore at once.

Monitor the child's behavior around, and attitude toward, your husband. When does she spend time alone with her father or stepfather? How does she respond when she comes home or when you ask about that time? Are there patterns to her mood or behavior after being with him?

Watch your child for telltale behaviors:

- A sexually abused child is very likely to act out sexually with other children. However, keep in mind that some sexual curiosity and play (peeking at one another's privates, for example) is also normal between small children. Don't overreact or shame your child in such situations. Calmly ask the child to explain what happened between her and the other child. If it seems innocent, it probably is. If the child appears disturbed or upset, however, let that be a red flag.
- A sexually abused child often withdraws from normal play activities and becomes preoccupied with sexual fantasies.[3]
- A sexually abused child often exhibits nervous habits, anxiety, slipping grades, loss of appetite, blank eyes or facial expression, and lack of childlike zest.

If you experience continued subtle misgivings but no evidence of molestation, confide in a trusted and qualified person, such as a counselor, pastor, or trusted friend. Ask for advice on how and if to confront your husband.

Talk with your child about your concern. Most child molesters make the threat of hurting the child or the other parent if the child tells about the abuse. Your child may fear that you'll be hurt if she confides in you. First seek advice from a counselor about what to ask and say, then look for the right moment to speak. Be sure to use age-friendly language, and if you haven't already talked with your child about what abuse is and what to do if it happens, do so now.

If you find evidence that your husband is abusing your child, you must report the abuse to the state's division of child welfare. This is the law. If you do not, you are guilty as well as your husband, as you knew about the abuse but did nothing to protect your child.

Get help for your child. An abused child often feels responsible for the abuse. Your child will need constant reassurance that he did nothing to cause Dad to molest him. Tell him that while his father loves him, he is sick and needs help to get well.

6. What if my husband suffers from a mental illness or chemical imbalance but won't seek treatment or stay on his medication?
Untreated mental illnesses and/or chemical imbalances make for an unpredictable marriage relationship and home life. God's mercy is rich toward you as well as toward your husband. Don't try to carry this burden alone or tell yourself that you are a failure if you need help coping. Enlist help from a counselor, pastor, friend, or family member. Being faithful also means being real. That usually means admitting that our power is limited. We need grace extended to us by others as well as by God.

In addition,

- Assess whether you should admit your husband to a treatment center, adult day care facility, or a hospital. If you think he is a danger to himself or others, you should certainly consider this. Call a professional who has experience working with the mentally ill to help you assess the severity of the situation.

- Consider doing an intervention with family members and friends who have observed your husband's erratic behavior or mood swings. If you go this route, be sure to enlist the help of a professional who can guide and oversee the intervention. Interventions can be effective in helping people recognize that they aren't coping as well as they thought and that they need help.

- Assess whether your children should see a counselor to help them process their father's behavior. Are your children able to function normally day to day without undue stress? Can they have friends over without fear of their father's disturbing mood swings? Are they in any way being demoralized by witnessing his uncontrolled outbursts or chronic depression and cynicism? If you answer yes to these questions, your children may need more support and counsel than you can offer alone. If counseling isn't feasible, consider hooking your child up with a mentor of some kind or a Big Brother or Big Sister.

- Educate yourself about your spouse's illness and find a support group of other women in your situation. Your spouse might be there for you one day or one moment, then suddenly not be there the next. Perhaps he will go through cycles or episodes of mental/emotional imbalance. The more you know about what to expect and why, the more grace you may be able to extend to him. He'll likely embarrass you in public, but you've got to be able to take it all in stride, or to at least ride it out.

- Take care of yourself. Explore your own interests and get involved in activities you enjoy.

Notes

INTRODUCTION

1. George Barna Research Online, Ventura, CA, December 21, 1999 @ www.barna.org.

CHAPTER 1

1. Teresa de Bertodano, editor, *Daily Readings with Mother Teresa* (London: Fount, 1993), 47.

2. Walter Kirn, "Should You Stay Together for the Kids?" *Time*, 12 September 2000, 76.

3. Zig Ziglar, "Family Happiness Is Homemade," *Family Concern*, Vol. 16, no. 2, Feb. 1992, n.p.

CHAPTER 2

1. Susan Page, *How One of You Can Bring the Two of You Together* (New York, NY: Boadway, 1998), 49.

CHAPTER 4

1. Warren Myers and Ruth Myers, *Pray: How to Be Effective in Prayer* (Singapore: Navigators, 1982), 166–7.

2. Adapted from David Kopp and Heather Kopp, *Praying the Bible for Your Marriage* (Colorado Springs: WaterBrook Press, 1999), 10–11.

CHAPTER 5

1. Dr. Kevin Leman, *Making Sense of the Men in Your Life* (Nashville, TN: Thomas Nelson, 2001).

CHAPTER 7

1. Walter Kirn, "Should You Stay Together for the Kids?" *Time*, 12 September 2000, 76.

2. Judith Wallerstein, Julia Lewis, and Sandra Blakeslee, "Fear of Falling," *Time*, 12 September 2000, 87.

3. Linda J. Waite and Maggie Gallagher, *The Case for Marriage: Why Married People Are Happier, Healthier, and Better off Financially*, (New York: Doubleday, 2000), 143-4.

4. Dennis Rainey, *One Home at a Time* (Colorado Springs: Focus on the Family, 1997), 149.

CHAPTER 11

1. John Welwood, *Journey of the Heart* (New York: Harper Collins, 1990), 75.

CHAPTER 12

1. Henry Cloud, "The Simple Scoop on Boundaries," Cloud Townsend Resources, 2000 @ www.cloudtownsend.com.

2. Ibid.

CHAPTER 14

1. Anne Wilson Schaef, *Meditations for Women Who Do Too Much* (San Francisco: Harper San Francisco), 6 August 1990.

CHAPTER 15

1. Mike Mason, *The Mystery of Marriage* (Sisters, OR: Multnomah Publishers, 1985), 37.

Chapter 16

1. Randy Alcorn, *Lord Foulgrin's Letters* (Sisters, OR: Multnomah Publishers, 2000), 178.

Chapter 17

1. Anne Wilson Schaef, *Meditations for Women Who Do Too Much* (New York: Harper San Francisco, 17 July 1990).

2. Oswald Chambers, *My Utmost for His Highest* (New York: Dodd, Mead and Company, 1935), 2.

Chapter 19

1. Larry Crabb, *The Marriage Builder* (Grand Rapids, MI: Zondervan, 1982), 55.

2. Ibid., 60.

3. Ibid., 113.

Chapter 20

1. Jim McGuiggan, *Celebrating the Wrath of God* (Colorado Springs: WaterBrook Press 2001), 104–5.

Chapter 21

1. Richard Foster, *Celebration of Discipline* (San Francisco: Harper and Row, 1978), 9.

Chapter 22

1. Bruce Wilkinson, *Experiencing Spiritual Breakthroughs* (Sisters, OR: Multnomah Publishers, 1999), 156.

CHAPTER 23

1. Larry Crabb, *The Marriage Builder* (Grand Rapids, MI: Zondervan, 1982), 70–71.

2. Gary Chapman, *Loving Solutions* (Chicago: Moody, 1998).

CHAPTER 24

1. Kristen Johnson Ingram, *Blessing Your Enemies, Forgiving Your Friends* (Liguori, MO: Liguori Publications, 1993), 25–6.

CHAPTER 25

1. Clifford L. Penner and Joyce J. Penner, *Restoring the Pleasure* (Nashville, TN: Word Publishing, 1993), 210.

2. Ibid., 216.

3. Ibid., 125.

CHAPTER 31

1. Richard Foster, *Celebration of Discipline* (San Francisco: Harper and Row, 1978), 167.

CHAPTER 33

1. Source unknown.

CHAPTER 35

1. Dan Allender, *Bold Love* (Colorado Springs: NavPress, 1992), 32.

2. Mike Mason, *The Mystery of Marriage* (Sisters, OR: Multnomah Publishers, 1985), 130.

CHAPTER 38

1. Margaret Becker, "In Search of Heroic Women," *Virtue*, May/June 1992, 28.

CHAPTER 40

1. Larry Crabb, *The Marriage Builder* (Grand Rapids, MI: Zondervan, 1982), 110.

APPENDIX

1. National Clearinghouse on Family Violence, "What Is Emotional Abuse?" @ www.hc-sc.gc.ca, 2001.

2. Adapted from Grace Ketterman, *Real Solutions for Abuse-Proofing Your Child*, (Ann Arbor, Michigan: Servant Publications, 2001), 81, 11–3.

3. Ibid., 11–3, 65–107.

Deb Kalmbach would love to hear from you.
Contact her at:

Rt. 1 Box 400–41
Winthrop, WA 98862

or e-mail her at:
debk@methow.com

Printed in the United States
by Baker & Taylor Publisher Services